Marketing & Economics

An integrated approach to making effective business
decisions in the world of global marketing

Sultan Kermally

Vernon Series in Business and Finance

VERNON PRESS

www.vernonpress.com

In the Americas:	*In the rest of the world*
Vernon Press	Vernon Press
1000 N West Street,	C/Sancti Espiritu 17,
Suite 1200, Wilmington,	Malaga, 29006
Delaware 19801	Spain
United States	

Vernon Series in Business and Finance

Library of Congress Control Number: 2016943287

ISBN: 978-1-62273-117-6

Cover elements designed by Freepik

This book is dedicated to my wife Laura and my children Jenny, Susan, Pete and Zara and my grandchildren Matthew, Anna and Eve.

My love and my 'Thank you' to them for their support.

Acknowledgements

I thank all writers and organisations quoted in my book and involved in economics and marketing for their contribution to my work. In particular Simon and Schuster, Pearson/Prentice Hall, The MIT Press, Europe Direct, American Marketing Association, Mises Institute. I would also like to thank my anonymous reviewer for his/her constructive comments to my draft copy of this book and Vernon Press Publishers for accepting to publish my book. Thank you also to all my Economics and Marketing students for adding value to my teaching experience.

I have provided acknowledgements of the ideas and concepts and comments I have used and explained in this book from various sources on-line and off line. Where I have failed to do so I very much regret the omissions.

About the author

Dr. Sultan Kermally is an Economics graduate and a Chartered Marketer. He holds degrees in Geography, Economics, Sociology and Law, Diploma in Finance & Accounting, Diploma in Marketing, Certificate in Further Education, Certificate in on-line teaching and Certificate in Mentoring. He is also the Fellow of the Chartered Institute of Marketing.

He has conducted management training for well-known organisations in the UK, the Netherlands, Belgium, France, Italy, Greece, Austria, the Middle East, Hong Kong, Kyrgyzstan and Tajikistan. He has gained insight into international business perspectives as well as multi-cultural perspectives as far as delivering services and products are concerned.

He has been involved in teaching various undergraduate modules and MBA modules for the Open University Business School, Durham University Business School, Chartered Management Institute, Oxford Brookes University and Laureate/University of Liverpool.

For several years he held senior academic positions in Scotland and thereafter senior directorship positions at Management Centre Europe (Brussels), London Business School and the Economist Conferences (The Economist Group) based in London.

At Management Centre Europe and again at the Economist, he spent some time working with well-known management gurus including late Peter Drucker, Michael Porter, Tom Peters, Richard Pascale, Philip Kotler, Don Schultz, Rosabeth Moss Kanter, Tony Buzan and Benjamin Zander.

Books by the author:

- *'Total Management Thinking'* (1996). Butterworth Heinemann.
- *'Management Ideas'* (1997). Butterworth Heinemann.
- *'Managing Performance'* (1997). Butterworth Heinemann.
- *'When Economics Means Business* - the New Economics of Information Age (1998). FT Management.
- *'Management Toolkit'* (1999). Thorogood.
- *'E-business Energy: Unleashing Knowledge for Competitive Advantage'* (2001). John Wiley.
- *'Effective Knowledge Management: A Best Practice Blueprint'* published under the umbrella of CBI fast track. The book was published by John Wiley in April, 2002.
- *'Gurus on Marketing'* (2003). Thorogood.
- *'Developing and Managing Talent'* (2004). Thorogood
- *'Gurus on 'Managing People'* (2005), Thorogood.

Table of Contents

Chapter Four Pricing. An important aspect of marketing mix

List of diagrams

List of tables

List of acronyms and other initials used

A.I.D.A.   Attention, Interest, Desire, Action.

B2C   Business to Customers.

B2B   Business to Business.

B.R.I.C.S.   Brazil, Russia, India, China South Africa.

CPA   Customer Profitability Analysis.

CLV   Customer Lifetime Value.

CPV   Customer Perceived Value.

CRM   Customer Relationship Marketing. Customer Relation-
              ship Management.

DMU   Decision Making Unit.

EEC   European Economic Community.

EPA   Environmental Protection Agency.

EU   European Union.

EDI   Electronic Data Interchange.

EVCO   Economic Value of the Customer Organisation.

FMCG   Fast Moving Consumer Goods.

4Cs   Customer Value, Cost to Customer, Convenience,
              Communication.

GATT	General Agreement on Tariffs and Trade.
GVCs	Global Value Chains.
IMF	International Monetary Fund.
ITO	International Trade Organisation.
MGI	McKinsey Global Institute.
NAFTA	North American Free Trade Agreement.
PwC	Price Waterhouse Coopers.
S.T.E.E.P.	Sociological, Technological, Economic, Environmental, Political.
SWOT	Strength, Weaknesses, Opportunities and Threats.
TQM	Total Quality Management.
USA	United States of America.
WTO	World Trade Organisation.

Introduction

"It is no crime to be ignorant of economics, which is, after all, a specialized discipline and one that most people consider to be a 'dismal science.' But it is totally irresponsible to have a loud and vociferous opinion on economic subjects while remaining in this state of ignorance."

Murray N. Rothbard. (1)

This book aims to bring the disciplines of economics and marketing together in order to highlight the integrative nature of these two subjects.

The world has changed dramatically over the last four decades. Sociologically, technologically, economically and politically speaking, diffusion of thoughts, changing values and philosophies are taking place thus reinforcing globalisation process in relation to various business operations and activities. In the spirit of continuous improvement, we have to examine various disciplines and subjects in order to make them more meaningful in relation to the world we live in.

This book focuses its attention on economics and marketing. The key basic principles, theories and issues of economics are selected and they are integrated with key elements and principles of marketing. Marketers, in conventional as well as in digital world, are encouraged to integrate marketing with economics in order to make successful and effective business decisions.

Marketing and Economics are subjects dealing with business – business of private firms, not-for-profit organisations and that of Government. Economics involves allocation of scarce resources. Scarcity in economics is relative scarcity, scarcity in relation to demand.

Globally the economic climate is changing significantly. There was a huge economic and financial crisis during the period of 2007 - 2008 facing few countries in the global world. After the 2007-2008 economic/financial crisis some of the countries like USA and UK were making good economic progress. However, at present some economic downfall is being experienced in some countries like Japan and China. In the Economist Newspaper published on 5th. February, 2016, it was stated that almost a quarter of world's GDP now comes from countries with negative interest rates.

Marketers have constantly to keep in touch with micro- economic as well as macro-economic situation of the globalised world in order to be able to use their management skills and the tools effectively.

Marketing is about satisfying the expressed needs of customers that is meeting demand. Many principles, concepts and models found in marketing are grounded in economics.

Economics to some extent appears to be very narrow in its approach. For example, in exploring consumers' preferences the subject does not explore in depth these preferences. Whereas in marketing, understanding these preferences enable marketers to design effective marketing communication and target the segments to satisfy demand. In the past few years there has been significant development in using digital media to focus on consumer demand and consumer preferences and expectations.

The two subjects, namely Marketing and Economics are brought together to show their interrelationship and relevancy of understanding both of them properly in order to practise economics and marketing effectively. This is the marriage of necessity rather than convenience.

The Circular Economy

Economics deals with scare resources. Resources are diminishing and some resources get wasted. Some organisations now have undertaken ground level innovation to pilot business model and framework in relation to Circular Economy.

What is Circular Economy? According to Wrap (2016):

"A circular economy is an alternative to a traditional linear economy (make, use, dispose) in which we keep resources in use for as long as possible, extract the maximum value from them whilst in use, then recover and regenerate products and materials at the end of each service life." (2)

According to The Guardian 2016,

"Our relationship with the products and services we purchase could be radicalised under a circular economy. What if we didn't buy the goods we use, but instead favoured access and performance over ownership? The 'pay per use' contractual agreements associated with smartphones for example could be extended to standard goods such as washing machines, clothes and DIY equipment." (3)

The Circular Economy is an alternative to 'make-use-dispose' linear economy. Analysis by McKinsey estimates, shifting towards circularity could add $1 trillion to the global economy by 2025 and create 100,000 new jobs within the next five years.

In 2014, The European Commission published a document entitled: *"Towards Circular Economy: A zero waste programme for Europe."* In it, the Commission outlined key business processes and operations that need to be innovated in order to achieve sustainable growth and the publication also highlighted the role played by small businesses and consumers. The marketers have to be aware of such innovative developments envisaged to take part in our economy and subsequently global economy.

At recent World Economic Forum held in January, 2016, the topic of Circular Economy was raised with specific reference to the way entrepreneurs could lead in creating such a business model.

In the author's view such development will change the nature of classical economic system though consideration still has to be given to the basic economic principles and their adaptation to keep up with the changing global world.

Why focus on the discipline of Economics?

Philip Kotler the father of modern Marketing trained as an economist. Three of his professors were Nobel Prize Economists – Milton Friedman, Paul Samuelson, and Robert Solow. In his interview with Niaz at eTalks which took place on 26th. April, 2013, he said:

> *"When I was offered a position to teach either economics or marketing at the Kellogg School of management at Northwestern University, I chose to teach marketing so that I could show that it was a branch of economic science."* (4)

In relation to writing his latest book '*Confronting Capitalism*' published in 2015 by The Amacom, he said in response to an interview question:

> *"Although most of my writing and teaching have centered on marketing, I always approached marketing as an economist hoping to help firms maximize their long run sales and profits."* (5)

In 'The Economist' January 10th-16th, 2015 UK publication, there were two articles, one on '*Economics evolves – A long way from dismal*' (page 8) and the other one on '*Silicon Valley economist -Meet the market shapers*' (page 67). The first article stated that microeconomists powered by data is shaping each tech firms. Silicon Valley firms employ economists to use data to find out behaviour of customers.

In the second article 'The Economist' explained how organisations are now using economists to help them solve real life problems.

The article concluded:

"In adopting products to match supply and demand, this new breed is injecting economics into the structure of Silicon Valley firms. While they are too busy to realise it such firms are also providing the best defence of economics against it critics. Far from being unrealistic and out of touch, the role of chief economist will design the way that the firm works." (6)

Book Structure

The book is divided into ten chapters. The topics of these chapters reside into two main components of economics, namely **demand and supply**. Chapter one focuses on demand – customers. Chapters two, three, four, five, six, seven and nine focus on firms (supply) and their efforts to meet demand effectively. Chapter 8 provides the global landscape within which demand and supply function and chapter ten on customer relationship and engagement, the focus of marketing philosophy.

The book is based on my understanding of economic concepts, principles, issues and philosophy and approach in marketing. In spite of rapid expansion of various technological media at our disposal, the understanding of the integration of marketing and economics becomes very essential.

Note for Readers

References: The author has deliberately used some key reference material– (accessed from websites and from various other sources)- in order to emphasise the basic nature of economics and basic principles and practice of marketing. Such combination in the author's view reinforces the key points he wishes to emphasise in order to show integrative approach to marketing and economics in practice. The author has cited some key authors who have put forward key concepts and principles in marketing and economics and some website sources which would be very useful to marketers.

The Nature of Demand-Consumer Behaviour and Preferences

What is demand?

Economics studies how societies use scarce resources to produce valuable commodities and distribute them among different people.

Resources are scarce so it is important to decide **what, how and for whom** to produce in order to satisfy needs and wants. Scarcity in Economics is relative scarcity i.e. scarcity in relation to demand. Given unlimited needs and wants, it is important for the society to use resources efficiently and effectively. Whatever is produced to satisfy demand there is always an **opportunity cost** involved. This is the cost of not producing other goods. Because of relative scarcity, economics put emphasis on element of **choice.**

In economics, a distinction is made between demand and want or desire. If an individual desires to have an expensive car then it does not constitute demand as far as Economics is concerned because in Economics demand is 'effective demand, i. e. demand backed by money. If an individual does not have financial means to purchase a car, he/she desires then in economic sense there is no demand for a car. If there is no demand, there will not be a need for an organisation to incur costs to produce a car. This is very important point for marketers to understand that it is not possible to create a demand by advertising or by investing in different forms of marketing communication if financial or other resources backing the demand are lacking.

When we talk about demand, we always mean demand backed by resources be they cash or credit availability.

Economists have formulated a **law of demand**. According to this law, generally speaking, people buy more of something when the price of that product or commodity falls and buy less when the price increases. The quantities demanded of a particular product change according to price changes. If we were to present, this law in a graphical form it will look like diagram 1.

Chapter one. Diagram 1. Price and quantities demanded.

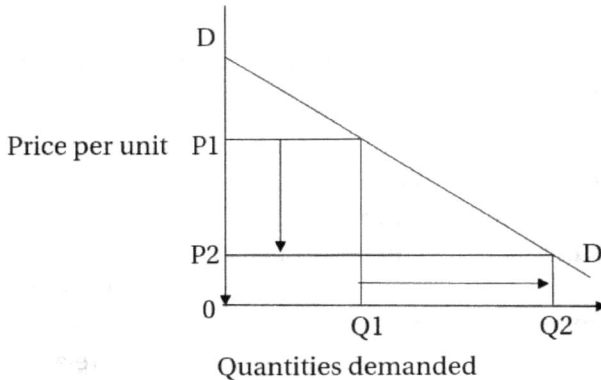

When the price is P1, quantities demanded are Q1. When price falls to P2, quantities demanded increase to Q2. The relationship between price and quantities demanded is **inverse relationship**. This means the two variables, price and quantities demanded move in opposite directions. The demand curve generally slopes downwards from left to right.

Individuals' demands are aggregated to determine market demand. Because financial resources to back demand are limited, in practice, individuals are forced to make choice in deciding what and how much to buy. There is always an opportunity cost involved in making purchasing decisions. An opportunity cost is a sacrificed alternative. Consciously or unconsciously, consumers have scale of preference and it is assumed that individuals make their decisions according to their **scale of preference**.

The knowledge of the existence of scale of preferences provides an opportunity for marketers to influence consumers' purchasing decisions. This is done by advertising and designing effective marketing communication campaigns with conventional and digital media available.

Consumers have to decide how to obtain maximum satisfaction from their limited resources. Their decision is influenced by the price they have to pay and to equate price with the value they are going to derive from their purchase.

Changes in quantities demanded and changes in demand

Economists distinguish between changes in the quantities demanded and changes in demand.

Changes in quantities demanded depend on the changes in price. Generally speaking, when price increases, quantities demanded decrease and when price drops, quantities demanded increase. **The demand curve does not shift**.

Changes in demand as such bring about changes in demand curve as shown in diagram 2. Changes in demand come about as a result of changes in income, tastes, prices of related goods and services, advertising and various levels of expectations. If there is an increase in demand the demand curve moves to the right from DO to D1 and if there is decrease in demand, the demand curve moves to the left from DO to D2.

Chapter one. Diagram 2. Shifting of demand curves.

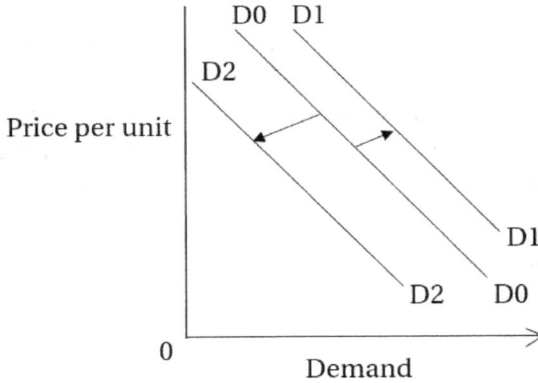

Marketers have to pay attention to the distinction between changes in quantities demanded and changes in demand in order to formulate their effective marketing strategies conventionally and digitally.

Price elasticity of demand and marketing mix strategy

The slope of the demand curve depends on the nature of the good in question. Some goods have very steep demand curve whereas other goods have gentle sloping demand curve. The economists explain this by introducing the concept of **price elasticity of demand**. According to the law of demand, when the price of the good falls, the quantities demanded increase but the degree of the responsiveness of increase depends on the nature of the good. For example, if price falls by 10%, the quantities demanded will increase but this increase may only be in the region of 6%. On the other hand, in relation to the nature of the good involved, the increase in the quantities demanded could be in the region of 15%.

Price elasticity of demand is consumers' responsiveness to price changes. When a 10% fall in price leads to a 15% increase in the quantities demanded then the economists say the price elasticity of the good in question is 1.5 (increase in quantities demanded divided by the increase in price; 15/10=1.5).

If, on the other hand the price falls of 10% leads to increase in the quantities demanded by 8%, then the elasticity of the good in question is 0.8 (8/10).

When the price elasticity is more than 1, the good is termed to be elastic in demand. When the elasticity is less than 1, the good is termed to be inelastic in demand.

What is the significance of price elasticity of demand to a marketer or to a business?

The concept of price elasticity of any product is a relative concept, that is, it is relative to price range, type of good on offer, culture and so on. It is, therefore, important to find out about price elasticity of demand of a product before formulating pricing strategy. Price is one of the key components of marketing mix.

Price elasticity of demand impacts on revenues generated by changing price. If the product has elastic demand, then an increase in price will reduce the total revenue generated and decrease in price will increase total revenue generated as shown in the examples below:

Example 1

Price:£10.00 per unit. Quantities demanded at this price are 5000 units. Total revenue generated at this price is £50000.

Price increases by 10%. New price is £11 per unit. Quantities demanded decrease to 4400 (decrease of 12%). Total revenue will be £ 48400.00.

Price decreases by 10%. New price now is £9.00 per unit. Quantities demanded increase to 5600 (increase of 12%). Total revenue is £ 50400.

Generally speaking, assuming all other things remain the same, goods with elastic demand will bring more revenue when price is reduced and less revenue when price is increased.

Good with inelastic demand will tend to do the opposite. When price is increased it will bring in more revenue and when price is decreased it will reduce the total revenue. This will happen within the certain price range.

Example 2

Price is £10.00 per unit. Quantities demanded are 5000 units. Total revenue at this price is £50000.

Price increases by 10% to £11.00 per unit. Quantities demanded decrease to 4600 units. Total revenue increase to £50600.

Price decreases by 10% to £9.00 per unit. Quantities demanded increase to 5400. Total revenue decrease to £48600.00

It is possible for price elasticity of a good to vary between individuals depending on their incomes, culture and also on the time factor. For example, if we consider price elasticity of electricity, the demand for electricity during the day time may be inelastic compared to evenings or week-ends. The electricity company, therefore, can formulate price strategy to charge more during the day (increase revenue) and less during the evening or week-ends (increasing the revenue).

The other aspect in relation to looking at the demand of certain goods and services relate to **income elasticity of demand**. This is the relationship between a change in quantity demanded for good X and a change in real income. It is measured by dividing percentage in quantity demanded by percent change in income. Some goods known as **normal goods** have a positive income elasticity of demand. Other goods known as **inferior goods** have a negative income elasticity of demand. A firm can forecast sales volume and sales revenue based on knowing the measurement of income elasticity of demand of the goods it is dealing with. Income elasticity of demand plays key role in making effective pricing decisions of goods and services.

The price elasticity of demand and income elasticity of demand enable the marketers to practise **revenue management strategy**. Revenue management incorporates the practice of charging different prices for the same product to different segments or the same segments depending on the value they put on the product. Numerous articles have been written on rate fences and revenue management strategy over the last few years. Weisman and Kulick (2010) (7) stated that different prices can be charged for the same service and Kimes and Wirtz (2003) (8) looked at the acceptability of the revenue management practice. Rate fences are created to enable consumers to pay high prices on the basis of service characteristics or value they put on the product.

Rate fences can either be physical or non-physical. **Physical fences** reflect tangible differences in the product or service, for example, room with a lovely view outside commanding high price compared to a room without such a view commanding low price. Effectively, rate fences change the nature of the product and its associated demand. **Non-physical fences** relate to the different prices charged for the same service or a good depending on the timing of the purchase.

One generally finds it is relatively cheaper to book holidays to go abroad during school times than during the school holidays. This is one of the reasons why some families take their children out of the schools to go on holidays during school times much to the annoyance of the schools and the government.

To come up with marketing strategies to capture demand and then to manage revenue flows depend on understanding of consumer needs, their preferences and their perceptions. Marketing is not just about meeting consumer needs but also influencing consumer perceptions. This is important if one wants to focus on **consumer engagement**.

Consumers in digital marketing world perceive some characteristics of technology as beneficial in engineering his or her online shopping activities. The author, for example, has his own perceptions nowadays of the value of using the web to make his purchases. These perceptions are influenced by the types of media available relating to different types of goods and services. Consumers also now have recommendations and suggestions supplied by their peers. Some experts now talk about "digital youths" who make their purchasing decisions by using various digital media.

How do consumers/customers make purchasing decisions?

From an Economics perspective, consumers make decisions on the value they derive from their purchases. The question which is often asked by the prospective consumers is 'is it worth it?' This reflects value proposition of consumers. Marketers have to pay special attention to value proposition they incorporate when they promote their products or services in various advertising channels and digital media.

Price vs. Value

When customers buy goods or services, in most cases price is not the only consideration. Buyers consider their total marketing experience. The most important aspect of consumer buying behaviour is their perception of what benefits the product or service is going to give them. In other words, it is the perceived benefits that constitute value.

According to Kotler and Keller (2009),

"Customer perceived value (CPV) is the difference between the prospective customer's evaluation of all the benefits and all the costs of an offering and the perceived alternatives. Total customer benefit is the perceived monetary value of the bundle of economic, functional and psychological benefits customers expect from a given market offering because of the products, services, personnel and images involved..." (9)

The author came across the following piece but unfortunately he cannot remember the source:

"There is the old story of the barber who had a very good business giving $15 haircuts. One day another barber set up across the road from him and put a sign up in the window boasting "$5 Haircuts Here." The first barber did his sums and knew he could not compete on price. His solution? He countered with his own sign - "We Fix $5 Haircuts."

Now there's someone who knows the difference between price and value.

Psychological factors play key role in understanding how consumers make buying decisions. Marketers need to understand **who, what, why, when and where** of consumer buying process.

Consumers make purchases to satisfy their needs. Basic needs consist of food, shelter and clothing, and some people now even include mobile phones (yes indeed)! These needs are referred to as physiological needs. Beyond these needs are socio-psychological needs such as needs to reflect their social status. Economists classify these needs as necessities and luxuries.

The factors affecting consumer buying behaviour can be divided into internal factors and external factors. Internal factors relate to consumers' perception and personality. Perception is the process by which we see ourselves and the world we live in. When a marketer is promoting products or services, what matters is the way the consumers perceive the benefits derived from these products and services. What consumers perceive, they expect to receive.

The process of perception involves **exposure** (sensing stimuli), **attention** (recognising the nature of stimuli), **awareness** (making stimuli meaningful) and **retention** (retaining what we have created in our mind).

When a cream is promoted to emphasise the effect it has to remove facial wrinkles, consumers are attracted to this product (**exposure**). What does this product do? (**Attention**). It will remove wrinkles under my eyes and on my cheeks (**awareness**) and I now have product information in my head (**retention**).

Personality depends on the values, culture, and education of the consumers. Consumers' personalities change over time depending on the nature of personal growth. These days modern consumers show preferences and concerns in relation to ethical and environmental issues. Such preferences and concerns impact on the goods and services they demand.

Consumers nowadays initiate search process via various technological methods available to find information that would help them satisfy their needs. The buying behaviour presented by some market researchers involves the following five stages:

Stage one: Recognising needs. Determining needs.

Stage two: Searching to find out where and how to satisfy these needs.

Stage three: Evaluating various options to use available resources to get most value of satisfying these needs.

Stage four: Making a decision to purchase.

Stage five: Evaluating the experience after purchasing/ consumption for future decisions.

Nowadays digitisation plays a key role in going effectively through various stages mentioned. In practice most of the time consumers often go through these stages without being aware of specifically going through these stages.

The author's daughter who is 15 years old has recently decided to buy a make-up set for herself through on-line media. When he asked her how she has arrived at the decision as to what and where to buy the product, she informed him the 'googlisation' of her decision process. She conducted research on her mobile phone getting all the necessary information she wanted and based her decision to purchase her makeup set accordingly.

Demand: Ethical and environmental considerations

Some modern consumers are also influenced by ethical and environmental considerations. They now have to consider how goods are produced, what are the raw materials used, how safe and healthy are the products before they make buying decisions.

For example, demand for confectionaries is now influenced by the artificial additives added to products. Some additives harm children's health in the long run. Confectionary producers now remove artificial additives from sweets. Consumer pressure groups would like to see legal ban imposed on certain E-number additives.

Consumers also now pay attention to whether producers of products in the developing countries are disadvantaged by getting a poor deal from organisations which source materials and goods to satisfy consumer demand. We see 'The fair-trade mark' campaigns in many countries now. The FAIRTRADE Mark is an independent mark consumer label which appears on products as in independent guarantee that disadvantaged producers in the developing world are getting a better deal.

According to Fairtrade organisation,

"Fair Trade is about better prices, decent working conditions and fair terms of trade for farmers and workers." (10)

"The Fairtrade Foundation is an independent certification body which licenses the use of the FAIRTRADE Mark on products which meet international Fairtrade standards. This independent consumer label appears on products to show that disadvantaged producers are getting a better deal from trade. Today, more than 1.5 million people – farmers and workers – across more than 74 developing countries benefit from the international Fairtrade system." (11)

Fairtrade taps into a public awareness of the need to support producers and public demand for ethically sources goods, at the same time as allowing retailers to give their public image a boost.

Eating places like Starbucks, Pret a Mange are now running major advertising campaigns in most of their stores across the UK, telling consumers about how its products are sourced and made.

Pressure is also put on clothing manufacturers to develop a range of ethical clothing as a result of pressure of consumers who would like to satisfy their needs by demanding products produced ethically. Consumers who demand clothing now want to know about the way clothes are made.

In considering environmental consideration do take note of situations where some organisations make claims of producing goods or services with environmental benefits but in practice they may fail to substantiate their claims. This some experts have termed as **Greenwashing** practice. Greenwashing can make a company appear to be more environmentally friendly than it really is.

Volkswagen: Recent scandal

One of the most reputable car manufacturers company, Volkswagen has been accused of cheating its customers. According to BBC News Volkswagen has *"manufactured cars which has device in diesel engines that could detect when they were being tested, changing the performance accordingly "been dubbed the "diesel dupe. "* The Environmental Protection Agency (EPA) found that many VW cars being sold in America had devices in diesel engines that could detect when they were being tested, changing the performance accordingly to improve results. The German car giant has since admitted cheating emissions tests in the US.

It has now been found that this software device is also related to cars in Europe.

The buying decision by businesses in the private sector

The buying decision within a firm, other than a very small enterprise or public sector organisation is unlikely to be an individual. Normally it will be decision-making unit (DMU). The people within this Unit according to some writers are likely to include:

The user who probably has initiated the enquiry and will have particular needs and requirements.

The influencer (a technical adviser) who will assist in ensuring that the user's needs are met.

The buyer with the formal authority to authorise an order and who may also have certain conditions that must be met. In some organisations, especially in the public sector or where the purchase involves an amount over a particular sum, the buyer may have to obtain an approval from another person in the organisation.

The gatekeeper who controls the flow of information and the entry of salespeople.

Forecasting demand to formulate marketing strategy

Based on the above five-stage model of consumer buying process which is associated with concept of demand in economics, marketers have to conduct market research if they have to be successful in satisfying consumer needs.

They need to gather appropriate information on different segments of consumers and their associated needs and on their purchasing habits. In addition, marketers have to monitor trends and megatrends within the environment in which they do business.

Effective information gathering and analysis will enable marketers to forecast aggregate demand and plan their production to meet consumer needs. Market demand is an aggregate demand applying to a specific customer group in a specific geographical area. For example, marketers may want to forecast demand for beauty cosmetic products for a group of women between ages 18 and 38 in India. Forecasters may want to estimate not only current market demand but forecast potential market demand in order to prepare strategy to forecast future sales and or to formulate marketing penetration strategy.

To understand the nature of demand and the types of customers, organisations now spend a lot of money trying to collect information on their existing and potential customers. Alan Wilson (2003) (12) identified four types of customer data:

1. Behaviour data derived directly from the purchasing behaviour of customers.
2. Volunteered data given by customers through, for example, registering on a website.
3. Profile data obtained by linking our database with other sources of information .
4. Attributed data which is extrapolated from the results of market research. Although held anonymously, the results of research on

a small sample of the database can be flagged against the entire database.

Database marketing consists of collecting information electronically on present and potential customers. The organisation is then ready to use this data meaningfully in order to formulate appropriate marketing strategy.

One of the companies that does this well is Kellogg's. See detailed explanation of the value of conducting market research to launch a new product (13).

Kellogg's carries out some detailed market research with consumers to discover their thoughts and feelings.

There are two main approaches to market research:

- Qualitative
- Quantitative

Qualitative research involves working in detail with a relatively small number of consumers e.g. observing and listening to them talking in small groups in which they discuss the brand, products, packaging, advertising ideas, etc. This qualitative research helps to assess consumers' perceptions e.g. by giving them pictures of possible new packaging and letting them give their views on the benefits of the product and reasons why they use fibre based cereals. The qualitative research helps Kellogg's to develop the concept of a family of fibre brands.

Once the qualitative market research was complete it was possible to test the concept through quantitative research. This involves using questionnaire and survey approaches with a much larger sample of targeted consumers.

Big Data

Nowadays we read a lot about Big Data. Big Data is a vast amount of structured and unstructured very complex and diversified data that is in existence. It requires new techniques and architecture to make use of it in business, economic and social environment. It is characterised by its **volume, verity, velocity** and **variety**. This type of data is generated by social media, various digital platforms, scientific instruments and networks.

Organisations like Google, Apple, Microsoft use Big Data to gather customer transactions. Big Data is becoming speedier and more complex as people use more digital tools and techniques. The McKinsey Global Institute estimates that data volume is growing 40% per year and will grow 40 x between 2009 and 2020. Big data will play key role for marketers when they consider branding their products and services, customisation and personalisation in terms of retaining customers and gaining customer loyalty.

Big Data is being stored and accessed by way of cloud computing. This means that massive amount of data is being stored and accessed on the internet instead of computer hard drive. The 'cloud' is being used as a metaphor for 'the internet.' According to Intel IT Center, *"cloud computing is an enabler for advanced analytics with big data."*

Evolution of marketing – from production to sales to customer's focus and digital Marketing

Economics has always paid attention to consumers and their needs and their scales of preference in explaining the concept of demand. Marketers, on the other hand, have not always focused on customers. The focus initially was on production (how and what to produce) rather than on what customers want.

Even though marketing can be traced back to vary ancient times, we would focus our attention on 18th century onwards. In the beginning marketing was primarily concerned with producing products and delivering services to satisfy consumer wants. According to

Adam Smith, in his book *'The wealth of Nations'* published in 1776, *'consumption is the sole end and purpose of production...'* Adam Smith (1776), *'The Wealth of Nations.'* The emphasis was also put on the interests of producers rather consumers. He wrote, *'It is not from the benevolence of the butcher, the brewer, or the baker, that we expect our dinner, but from their regard to their own interest.'* The society during Smith's time was held together by exchanges which were prompted by self-interest. This situation, focusing on commodities and producers, went on for a long time. Commodities were produced in order to satisfy consumer demand and it was the price mechanism which regulated what was produced and what was sold. The term 'market' during this period referred to the mechanism of bringing the producers and consumers together. It was an economic institution which kept buyers and sellers in close touch with one another and they were able to fix its price. This was a definition of market from economics perspective.

At the end of 19th century and at the turn of the 20th century, the focus of attention turned to producing commodities and extending trade locally and internationally. The concept of the market was broadened to incorporate exports and imports but the focus was still on markets rather than marketing. Gradually it began to be realised that demand consisted of more than simple purchasing power. Due to division of labour and other factors, there was an overproduction of goods and the producers sought to influence consumers buying behaviour in order to sell their products. They began to advertise their products and the focus on advertising reflected the nature of the commodities produced. In order not to face financial ruins, some producers got together and founded co-operatives to produce and distribute their produces effectively. As the economies grew, international trade extended and marketing developed in order to manage distribution channels at a distance. This was the beginning of marketing in a narrow sense.

Some experts on marketing have branded this period as represented by **'the commodity school of thought.'** According to this school, goods were classified as 'convenience goods' and 'emergency goods.' Gradually this classification was extended to include 'preference goods' 'speciality products' and 'shopping products.' The concept of marketing also began to evolve as producers began to apply techniques and practices in order to sell and distribute their goods. The emphasis was thus changing from production-orientation to sales-orientation. Businesses began to invest in developing channels of distribution and recruit salesmen to sell the products. Marketing was all about selling what was produced.

The 'marketing mix' concept as we know now consisted then mainly of product, place and price. Promotion was mainly in the form of advertising- poster advertising. This gave rise to the development of marketing communication. The mid-18th century to the mid-19th century was the Golden age of advertising facilitated by advances in the mechanisation of printing. From the pages of Harper's weekly – 1857-1872, one can find advertising of ice cream freezers, wringers, refrigerators, washing machines, toilet soaps and so on. In the United States, the advertising profession began in 1841.

Development of the postal system encouraged mail-order selling and mail-order advertising. In fact, if one delves into the detailed history of marketing, one comes across the concepts of mass communication, relationship marketing, repeat business were being discussed (Deja vu!). Producers of commodities were also beginning to take notice of socio-psychological factors affecting consumer buying behaviours. Numerous books were published on advertising dealing with campaigns, economics of advertising and the influence of psychological factors.

The 20th century was essentially the period of **sales-orientation**. The emphasis was to sell what was being produced. Direct communication to consumers, advertising and branding were beginning to dominate in order to sell goods produced. The marketing communication was aimed at consumers as well as business-to-business customers. Such practice and activities were evident throughout Europe.

From the beginning of 1900 and going up to the end of the Second World War, marketing was dominated by paying attention on distribution channels, advertising, branding and selling. When you consider the market dominance of the *Model T* car developed by Ford Motor Company, it was very short-lived. The emphasis was on selling and communicating how wonderful the M*odel T* was. Ford was very much **production-oriented company.**

Marketing communication was still not singled out as one of the dominant components of marketing. Advertising as a means of marketing communication was being used extensively to 'sell' products and services. Kellogg's, for example, placed its first advertisement in 1906 for Corn Flakes in six mid-western newspapers. By 1915, the company was spending one million dollars on national advertising.

Advertising also facilitated the extension of the Coca Cola brand from national to international dominance. The brand was extended to 44 countries by the outbreak of the Second World War.

In the 1950s many marketing theorists began to advocate a more managerial-based approach; thus began the managerial school of marketing. According to Professor Jagdish Sheth, one of the marketing gurus,

"Then marketing, like economics, became 'managerial' by which I mean that marketing became the job of a manager; this in turn led to the concept of the four 'Ps' of marketing." (14)

Managerial approach involved looking at the quantitative aspects of marketing analysis, market research and borrowing concepts from other disciplines particularly in the field of social sciences and management.

In the beginning of the 1960s, marketing communication was beginning to emerge as a prominent component of marketing process. Significant works were being done by academics and consultants in exploring consumer behaviour and finding out the effective way of communicating with consumers and customers. Even though researches were being conducted in the 1950s on socio-psychological factors affecting buying behaviour of consumers, they were not incorporated in marketing discipline as such.

The 1960s saw the emergence of the buying behaviour school of thought. The consumer buying decisions were incorporated in the marketing discipline and marketing communication was formulated to respond to these decisions. This was a shift of paradigm, getting marketers to change from inward-looking approach to outward-looking approach. Promoting goods in form of advertising and or branding and communicating the attributes of these goods to consumers and customers depended very much on the behaviour of consumers. The understanding of their behaviour would facilitate the effective formulation of communication media.

The effectiveness of marketing communication was boosted by the invention and development of radio and television. The 20th century witnessed the use and the growth of radio and television advertising. Companies were spending significant amounts of their money through agencies in renting airways to communicate to consumers. The first television advertisement created for Coca Cola was in November, 1950. The subsequent advertisement of Coca Cola brand used animation, stop motion and live actions to reinforce the attributes of the product. The attention was also paid to the words used as they were translated into many languages in order to enable the slogan to travel the world.

The mode of communication became important in conveying the message to consumers and customers. Humour and cartoons were used to capture the attention of the consumers. Advertising in the U.S.A. was more extensive than in Europe.

The emphasis was also beginning to shift from production and sales orientation to marketing orientation. This shift also reinforced the importance of broader marketing communication concept in marketing strategy. The leading marketing guru who advocated **market-orientation approach** was Professor Theodore Levitt of Harvard Business School. He advocated shifting the focus from product-orientation to consumer-orientation. His article 'Marketing *Myopia*' published in Harvard Business Review in 1960 was his landmark article exploring the importance of paying attention to customers. This article made companies realise that they were in a business of creating value for customers. This article created impetus in thinking in marketing terms.

According to Levitt (1960), (15) in mass marketing, what gets emphasised is selling and not marketing. Attention is generally paid to selling commodities in order to generate cash. Marketing on the other hand is about satisfying customers' needs. Detailed attention has to be paid to customer needs. Satisfying customers' needs is one of the key principles of Economics.

In Levitt's term, producers are occupied in providing information to customers about their Research and Development efforts. The information to customers is influenced by the assumption on the part of the companies that by providing information on technical aspects of products, superior products will sell themselves.

Paying attention to customers' needs and their satisfaction changes the focus of communication. Marketing-orientation approach provides information on how the products will meet customers' needs and provide satisfaction. Levitt also emphasised the need for companies to do more research on understanding their customers.

Despite Levitt's article, most companies still focused their efforts on selling their products and services. As competition intensified in the 1960s and 1970s more and more efforts were being made to sell products. Many organisations adopted very aggressive selling techniques. Companies were spending more and more money just to stand still.

Gradually some companies began to adopt marketing-oriented approach advocated by Theodore Levitt. They were 'forced' to adopt this approach because consumers were become increasingly sophisticated and products and services were becoming less and less differentiated.

Significant attention was being paid now not just to win customers but to retain customers. '**Customer retention**' and '**getting close to customers**' became the 'buzz words' of the marketing community. Tom Peters, one of the management gurus, wrote best-selling books advocating 'getting close to customers' 'developing customer obsession' and 'listening to customers.'

Companies have to design their marketing communication to convey the message that they were geared to delivering service excellence and that they valued their customers and took initiatives to create relationship with their customers.

Location of demand, supply and market. Focussing on marketing strategies

Dr. Igor Ansoff, known as the father of strategic management, had a profound influence in the field of strategic management and thinking. In relation to marketing he was famous for his matrix, a well-known marketing tool came to be known as '**Ansoff's Matrix.**' The matrix is a tool which enables businesses achieving growth through existing or new products or in existing or new markets.

The matrix offers strategic choices facing marketers in order to achieve their objectives. According to Ansoff, the matrix involves two dimensions, namely, product and market. There are four permutations:

1. Existing product/existing market.
(Marketing Penetration Strategy)

In this situation an organisation has an option of either doing nothing which means continuing its strategy to satisfy consumer demand or to choose to consolidate its current market position by focusing attention and initiating marketing activities in the area where it has competitive advantage or to choose to penetrate the market. Revenues could be increased by increasing its demand from existing and potential customers. The example would be Airline companies and supermarkets and Chain retailers initiating loyalty schemes to retain customers and to 'capture' demand for existing segments of customers.

2. New product/existing market.
(Product Development Strategy)

In this scenario the organisation has to invest in introducing new products to its existing market. The focus is to build on the existing knowledge to explore new opportunities identified by the company.

Over time all products pass through the product life cycle. An existing product matures; new developments are often introduced to extend the product life cycle. An example of such a strategy would be Unilever's introduction of the three-in-one dishwater tablets which replaced the need for separate salt, detergent and rinse agents.

This strategy also recognises how consumers' needs change over time and therefore, it becomes necessary to come up with new products to satisfy consumer needs but holding on to its existing customers.

3. Existing product/ new market.
(Market Development Strategy)

Here the organisation has to market its existing product in a new market to take advantage of a potential demand in a different region, country or segment. This is a market development strategy. This strategy also involves promoting new uses for an existing product and market segments.

Market development can be achieved through identifying potential user groups in the current market areas or seeking additional distribution channels in the present geographical areas.

4. New product/new market.
(Diversification Strategy)

The organisation in this situation has to pursue what is known as diversification strategy. The company can decide to come up with new products in order to satisfy emerging new needs of consumers. It can do this by acquiring new but unrelated business. Example here could be Apple Company introducing iPods to existing and new markets.

Ansoff's matrix enables businesses to look at their products and markets and to think of appropriate strategies for their business in order to gain and sustain competitive advantage. To do this they have to undertake consumer research in order to meet their existing and potential needs.

All four strategies involve forecasting. The forecaster can choose subjective or objective methods to make decisions. In practice, however, marketers can use a hybrid forecasting techniques mixing subjective and objective methods.

How can marketers influence demand?

Marketers influence demand by deploying various promotional campaigns conventionally and digitally. They include advertising through various media such as newspapers, television, radio, bill boards, mobile phones and on various digital media such as Facebook, Tweeter, Websites, digital audio and so on. The way advertising and marketing communication are used to influence consumer purchasing decisions are explained in chapters six and seven respectively.

Use of Digital marketing

The term digital marketing is being used a lot nowadays and in some cases some individuals feel that marketing today is all about managing the skill of digital marketing. Digital marketing, according to the author, has to incorporate and embrace basic principles of conventional marketing in keeping the focus of consumer interest and concerns paramount. Digital marketing uses a range of digital technologies in order to address consumers and their needs. It involves uses of internet, mobile phones, blogging, tweeting, e-advertising, videos and so on in order to establish communication with customers. According to Philip Kotler, the marketing guru, new digital technologies affect all of the 4Ps of marketing – price, product, promotion and place.

Digital marketing, whichever platforms and technological media marketers choose to deploy, has to focus on consumer needs and wants and enable consumers to make their own choice in order to enable them to satisfy their demand. Consumers in our present world have access to information all the time and in real time. Consumers have access to information from various sources including twitter, blogs, social media and so on, and the sources of information they gather come from a variety of people and platforms.

According to the Economist Newspaper dated August 29th. 2015 (pp 53), few months ago BMW advertised on WeChat which has over 500 million users. In terms of consumer classification, the advertisement was shown only to those who were considered potential buyers of expensive cars. Potential media advertising expenses have increased to $20 billion in 2015. Social platforms are increasing all the time and marketers have to keep ahead communicating with different segments of consumers.

One should not think about digital marketing as separate discipline from conventional marketing. The aim of this book is to show that digital marketers need to understand socio-economic aspect of the markets they are exploring and consider digital marketing as the part of whole marketing process. The focus of digital marketing is in the use of channels and methods in order to analyse marketing campaigns. These channels include the internet, mobile messaging, social media and so on.

The Nature of Supply – Organisational perspective in relation to marketing goods and services

Supply in Economics relates to the amount of goods and services produced in an economy in order to meet the demand. Supply involves cost of production. The extents to which producers are willing to use scarce resources to produce goods depend on the price the consumers are willing to pay for the goods. Like demand there is also a law **of supply** in Economics.

The law of supply states that at any particular time, more quantities are supplied as the price rises and less quantities are supplied as price decreases, assuming all other things remaining equal. Let us take an example of product X's price and supply situations. If price of product x is £10, the quantities supplied let us say for example would be 2000 units. If the price of that product goes up to £11, the quantities supplied would increase to 2500 units. If the price falls to £9, the quantities supplied would decrease to say 2000 units. **The relationship between price movement and quantities supplied is direc**t. In figure 3 when the price of the commodity falls from P1 to P2 the quantities supplied fall from QS1 to QS0. If price increases from P2 to P1 then the quantities supplied will increase from QS0 to QS1.

Chapter two. Diagram 3. Price and quantities supplied.

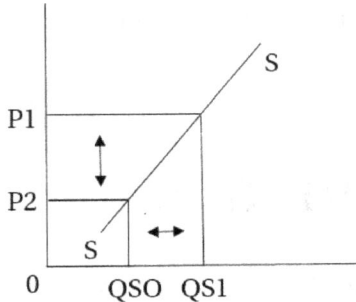

The aggregate of individual suppliers gives us the total market supply. Distinction should be made between **changes in quantities supplied and changes in supply**. Changes in quantities supplied come about because of changes in price. More is supplied at high price and less at low price.

Changes in supply (as opposed to changes in quantities supplied) come about because of changes in technological development, prices of inputs such as oil, changes in productivity (output per unit), number of producers and expectations of producers. Changes in supply involve changes in supply curves. Supply curve moving to the left showing decrease in supply or moving to the right indicating increase in supply.

Supply like demand also has the measure of price elasticity. **Price Elasticity of Supply** is defined as producers' responsiveness to price changes. If the proportionate change in quantities supplied divided by proportionate change in price is less than one, the supply is said to be inelastic. If the proportionate change in quantities supplied divided by proportionate change in price results in more than one, then supply is said to be elastic.

Elasticity of supply is affected by factors such as supply chain management, logistics, globalisation process and technological developments. All these factors impact upon the cost of supply. Because prices are determined by the interaction of demand and supply, the elasticity of supply plays an important part in determination of market price.

The Theory of the Firm and Outsourcing and Resourcing Decisions

In Economics, a firm is presented as an entity that operates in order to produce goods to meet consumer demand. This is the concept of supply at any given time. It is assumed that a supplier referred to as entrepreneurs behaves rationally i.e. that he or she is aiming to make greatest profit possible. Economists assume that entrepreneurs always produce each output as cheaply as possible and that each firm produces only one product. Factors of production used to produce output are assumed to be in infinitely elastic supply at their current price.

Based on these assumptions, Economists present their **theory of the firm**. According to this theory, entrepreneur will maximise profit when marginal cost of producing one unit of output equals marginal revenue of producing that unit of output.

This theory is very simplistic to apply in modern business. As far as back as 1937, Ronald Coase, a Nobel Prize Winner Economist presented the transaction Cost approach to the theory of the firm. (16) According to Coase, transaction cost refers to the cost of providing for some good or service through the market rather than having it provided from within the firm. The transaction involves search and information costs, bargaining and decision costs and policing and enforcement costs. Entrepreneurs have to weigh up the production and transaction costs associated with executing transaction within their firm (in-house production) against the production and transaction costs associated with executing the transaction in the market (outsourcing). Coase thus emphasised the internal working of the firm which becomes more relevant to the modern business.

Oliver Williamson who received 2000 Nobel Memorial Prize in Economic Sciences (17) took Coase's idea and developed it further. According to Williamson, the decision to in-source or outsource as such depends on the three variables. They are frequency, uncertainty and asset specificity.

Frequency: If there are activities that are not used frequently then the firms would source those activities. These activities would not use the core competencies within the organisation hence becomes cost effective to outsource to firms that have core competencies in this line of work.

Uncertainty: If dealing with outside firms involves uncertainty, for example, as to sustaining good relationship with contractor then the decision will be made to produce in-house.

Asset specificity: Where transactions involve assets that are only valuable to specific transaction, then it will have less value for alternative transactions. In this case, transaction costs will be less by outsourcing.

Transaction costs analysis has been used to explain the rationale behind vertical integration. But it can also be used to explain in-house sourcing against outsourcing decisions and rationale behind strategic partnerships and channel integration.

Economists and marketers have to understand not only the way organisations produce goods in order to meet demand, but how they produce such goods thus paying attention to the structure of the organisation and the nature of strategic and marketing alliances made to deliver goods to the consumers. All these activities reflect nature of transaction costs.

Outsourcing – Your place or mine?

Outsourcing is a way of sub-contracting a process or a function such as manufacturing, designing, market research, telemarketing, engineering to a third party. The outsourced process or function could be performed in-house but contracts are given to third parties to re-duce costs and because these outside companies may possess specialism.

Some companies outsource to focus their attention on core business and to make most of their competencies. The specialised company that handles the outsourced work has often specialised competencies and modern technology that a company could not afford to buy on their own.

The client organisation and the supplier of services enter into a contractual agreement that defines the outsourced services. When the transfer of services, process and functions is made to a supplier who lives in another country then it is referred as offshoring. Countries that benefit from outsourcing include China, India, Ireland, South Africa, Mexico, Russia, and the Czech Republic.

Almost every organisation outsources in some way. The outside firms that are providing the outsourcing services are third party providers known as service providers. The two most common forms of outsourcing are information technology outsourcing and business process outsourcing. Looking at their work a while ago, the well-known service providers included companies like IBM, EDS, Capgemini, and Accenture.

Outsourcing delivers the following benefits:

- **Cost savings.** Organisations that outsource focus on reducing costs in order to remain competitive. Outsourcing reduces overhead costs and investment in infrastructure.
- **Quality improvement.** Service providers, because they specialise in delivering services may have access to new technology and may be in a position to provide high quality services.
- **Capacity management.** Companies which outsource may not have adequate capacity to provide all the services and perform all business functions effectively.
- **Effecting change.** An organisation can use an outsourcing opportunity to initiate change.

- **Time to market:** Outsourcing can reduce the time to market by not focusing on all business functions. Thus they are able to deliver faster than usual at lower costs.
- **Time zone.** Multiple tasks can be performed sequentially over 24/7 period because of differences in time zones.
- **Growth.** Companies achieve growth and are able to develop and penetrate the markets without increasing their capacity.

It is reported that companies like Proctor & Gamble have outsourced IT infrastructure, facilities management and employee service to some service providers.

Some book publishers like Wolters Kluwer outsourced software development and editorial work to India and Philippines in order produce greater variety of books and journals more rapidly.

According to Philip Kotler, there is a lot of outsourcing going on. In some of his seminars he gave the example of Nike, an organisation many believe make shoes. However, according to Kotler, manufacturing of Nike shoes is done in the Far East. Nike designs shoes and market shoes.

Global Sourcing

The conventional wisdom in Economics is that manufacturers and retailers procure materials from domestic suppliers. This helps to maintain predictable deliveries and keep costs down and ensure control over supplier quality.

However, due to shrinkage in distance and technological developments in particular convergence of computing and telephony the world economy has undergone a radical transformation.

Due to intense competition, companies now are seeking materials from different parts of the world. Most companies now include global sourcing as a part of their procurement strategy. Global sourcing is about locating the right skills in the right location at the right costs.

It has been reported that Intel Corporation assembles most of its microchips in their subsidiaries based in China, Malaysia and Philippines. Nike subcontracts most of its manufacturing to independent producers in Thailand, Indonesia, Cambodia and Vietnam. Mattel sources materials in China, Hong Kong and Taiwan to make its toys. Barbie doll, for example, is the product of global sourcing from China, Taiwan, Japan and Hong Kong. Chrysler, US Car manufacturers orders its components from suppliers in Japan, Korea, Germany and other countries.

Cost is not the only consideration for global sourcing. In some cases, the material is only available abroad. Roche, Swiss pharmaceutical company had to source flu vaccine from China as the key ingredient was only available from China. The other reasons for global sourcing may be to acquire new technology or specialised skills or to meet quality requirements or simply to establish an alternative source of supply.

Global sourcing – ethical and environmental considerations

From demand perspective, consumers need and values change over time. Consumers now demand goods and services that are consistent with their value propositions. The focus now has shifted from consumer marketing to stakeholder marketing taking into consideration various pressure groups influencing consumers' needs and values. Suppliers have to take into consideration consumers' values in sourcing globally

The top outsourcing companies globally include Capgemini, Colliers International, Sodexo, Wipro Technologies, IBM and Accenture.

Suppliers beware!

Following are few examples taken from the past couple of decades of the attention suppliers had to pay to in sourcing and manufacturing finished products. Such examples have given rise to marketers paying attention to all the stakeholders rather than just the consumers:

- Nike was hit by a child labour row over the way it manufactured the balls used in FA Premier League matches. It was alleged that some of the balls may have been stitched by children in their homes. After complaints with from various pressure groups Nike sacked its supplier, Pakistani firm Saga Sports.
- Fisher-Price had to recall tens of thousands of toys sold in the UK amid concerns over excessive levels of lead in their paint. Globally they recalled almost a million Chinese-made plastic preschool toys over safety fears. The toys included Dora the Explorer, Big Bird and SpongeBob SquarePants characters.
- In 1995, New Persil Power detergent was criticised for damaging clothes. Company later paid compensation to claimants and the product was withdrawn.
- In 2004 Coca-Cola recalled Coca-Cola Desani brand in the UK, following a controversial launch. Traces of carcinogenic chemicals were found in the water brand.
- In 2006, U.S. Toy Co. Inc. in cooperation with the U.S. Consumer Product Safety Commission recalled thousands of children's Butterfly Necklaces. The clasps of the necklaces contained high levels of lead. Lead is toxic if ingested by young children and can cause adverse health effects.
- In 2007, Cadbury went through a major recall of some of their best selling products in the UK because the bars tested positive for traces of salmonella.
- In 2013 Walmart accepted clothing from banned Bangladesh factories. It warned suppliers that they adopt "zero tolerance policy" and they would stop trading with suppliers who would break their code of practice.

- In 2016 the Report was produced by indicating Britain's largest supermarket Tesco has "seriously breached" a legally binding code to protect grocery producers by prioritising its own finances over the fair treatment of its suppliers, a new report has found. The investigation was launched by the Groceries Code Adjudicator (the GCA) on 5 February 2015.

In addition, the following examples taken from the past few years illustrate the responsibilities modern suppliers have to face to take on board ethical and environmental considerations in order to satisfy consumers' needs.

- Major food products now have incorporated fair trade products into their offer.
- 3M manufacturing plan scaled down a wastewater treatment operation by half, simply by running cooling water through its factories repeatedly instead of discharging it after a single use.
- McDonalds have been criticised by various groups of contributing towards rising levels of obesity and other health problems. The company were forced to print nutritional facts on the packaging of its food. They also now offer some healthy food options such as salads and organic milk.
- Toyota have produced Prius Hybrid car that runs on petrol and battery to meet eco demands. This mode of production is followed by some other car manufacturers as well.
- Bodyshop takes a stance against animal testing and Lush only buys materials from suppliers who share their values.

Most of the organisations now have their own code of conduct practice in order to eliminate or minimise malpractices in business.

Offshoring and reshoring to be near to markets

Offshoring means a situation when an organisation 'offshores' its business operation from one country to another. Such operation could be its manufacturing activities, its accounting activities its technology or Research and Development. The advantages of off-shoring are similar to those for outsourcing. It is reported that more than 20% of American companies undertake some offshoring.

However, nowadays 'reshoring' is taking place by some organi-sations such as General Electric, Caterpillar and Ford Motor Com-pany. In fact, in some cases offshoring is now taking place from de-veloping countries to developed countries. Lenovo, a Chinese tech-nology company is now manufacturing in North Carolina, USA.

> *"The most prominent current example of the opportunities and risks of offshoring is the relationship between Apple and Foxconn. From a strategic point of view, the partnership could not be more successful. In 2010 Foxconn took a huge chance by investing billions of dollars in building enough capacity in China to manufacture Apple's iPhone on the scale required. It built a uniquely flexible and responsive supply chain for the American firm. On one recent occasion, according to a report in the New York Times, Apple redesigned the iPhone's screen at the last minute and Foxconn woke up its workers in the middle of the night to get the job done in time. "The reason Apple is what it is today is Foxconn," says a consultant in Taipei who prefers not to be named. The two companies, he says, are inex-tricably bound to each other."* (18)

On 19th January, 2013, in the article *'Here, There and Everywhere,* Tamzin Booth wrote: that organisations now are 'onshoring' in that the production is now moving to areas close to customers. China is now seen as a huge new market.

> *"Companies now want to be in, or close to, each of their biggest markets, making customised products and responding quickly to changing local demand. Pierre Beaudoin, chief executive of Bombardier, a Canadian maker of aeroplanes and trains, says the firm used to focus on cost savings made by sending jobs*

abroad; now Bombardier is in China for the sake of China."
(19)

In addition to supplying goods to meet demand, suppliers also have to consider two other issues which play significant role in the modern economy. They are (1) concern for quality (2) delivering good customer care.

Quality

According to some key marketing experts, in developing or designing a product, the supplier has to think about the product at three levels. The first level is the '**core product**' level incorporating all the benefits of the consumers. The second is the '**tangible product**' level. At this level the product assumes the characteristics of quality, features, packaging, styling and brand name. Finally, the supplier has to enhance benefits and make up an '**augmented product**.' At this stage the benefits are enhanced to meet customer needs and aspirations in relation to that product.

There are various studies that show that the perceived relative quality of a product or service is the single most important factor determining the long-term market share and profitability.

Consumers were demanding ever-improving standards and competition was becoming intense. The enthusiasm for quality came about because many organisations were finding it hard compete with Japanese products. Japanese goods in the form of cars and electronics penetrated Western home markets. Most organisations in the West were forced to consider implementing **Total Quality management (TQM)**.

TQM is concerned with continuous improvement in performance aimed at delighting customers. Quality gurus like Joseph Juran, Edwards Deming and Philip Crosby advocated adoption of TQM.

USA and Europe initiated various Quality awards to provide incentives to organisations to embark upon TQM process. In USA, the Malcolm Baldrige National Quality Award was instituted in 1987. To win a Baldrige Award, companies have to submit an application form describing their quality practices and performance in seven required areas. These areas are: leadership, information and analysis, strategic planning, human resource development and management, process management, business results and customer focus and satisfaction. The name of the Award was changed in 2010 to the Baldridge Performance Excellence Program which is managed by the national Institute of Standards and Technology, an agency of the US Department of Commerce.

Early winners have included companies like Motorola, Xerox, and General Motor's Cadillac Division. The award was considered as the most important catalyst for transforming business. The award winners share information on their performance and quality strategies with other US organisations. The awards are given annually to categories covering manufacturing, service, education, healthcare, small business and non-profit organisations.

In Europe, The European Quality Award was developed by the European Foundation for Quality Management. The foundation was originally set up by 14 leading Western European businesses in 1988. The award was based on how the results were achieved called 'enablers' and the results themselves. Enablers included leadership, people management, policy and strategy, resources and processes. The results focused on people satisfaction, customer satisfaction, impact on society and business results.

In addition to these awards, international quality standards such as ISO 9000 were set up to promote quality initiatives. There are numerous success stories of the companies which have achieved significant improvements as a result of adopting TQM.

Quality in service

The concept of quality is easy to apply when one is considering tangible goods but difficult if one is delivering service. The intangible nature of a service and the concept of human involvement make it particularly difficult to ascertain standards, expectations and consistency of approach.

Parasuraman, Zeithaml and Berry (1985), (20) presented the following determinants of service quality:

- Reliability: Consistency and dependability of service provision.
- Access: Is it a hassle to get a service or is it easily accessible?
- Credibility: Can the supplier be trusted?
- Security: Is service free from risk?
- Knowledge: Is the supplier conversant with customer's needs?
- Responsiveness: Is supplier responsive to customer's demands?
- Competence: Do employees of service provider have appropriate skills to satisfy customers and deliver service excellence?
- Courtesy: Are staff polite and considerate to customers?
- Communication: Has a company an effective communication channels?
- Tangibles: Do company's tangible attributes such as appearance of their buildings or their staff project good image?

Customers compare what they receive against what they expect to receive. If what they receive is below their expectation, then they would look for alternative supplier and vice versa. Customer expectation is influenced by past experience, reputation, word of mouth and all kind of advertising. In digital age customers explore various forms of platforms in order to improve the quality of their own research as the main objective here is to try to achieve high degree of satisfaction. Supplier's challenge is to manage customer expectation successfully.

Gaps in service design and delivery

Parasuraman, Zeithaml and Berry (1985) (21) identified four potential gaps in relation to service provider. Christopher Lovelock and Lauren Wright (2007) (22) subsequently refined and extended these gaps to seven following gaps:

1. The knowledge gap: What the supplier perceives customers want and what they actually want.
2. The standards gap: This arises as a result of management perception of quality and the perception of customer's expectation.
3. The delivery gap: Supplier's actual delivery standards falling short of specified delivery standards. Delivery promises are not met.
4. The internal communication gap: Not delivery according the standards reflected in advertising and by sales staff.
5. The perceptions gap: The difference between what customers perceive they have received and what in fact is delivered.
6. The interpretation gap: What supplier actually promised and what the customer thinks was promised.
7. The service gap: Difference between what customers expect to receive and what they perceive to have received.

Gaps damage relationships with the customers and they frustrate supplier's strategic objectives. If suppliers do their research properly and gather information to eliminate or minimise these gaps, they can 'lock in' particular segments of their markets.

Customer care

Customer care involves putting processes, people and systems in place to maximise customers' satisfaction. It should be the prime consideration of every business. Sales and long-term profitability depend on gaining and retaining customers and keeping them satisfied.

Factors that impact on customer care include the following:

- How well your product or service matches customer needs;
- The value for money you offer;
- Your efficiency and reliability in fulfilling customers' orders;
- The professionalism, friendliness and expertise of your employees;
- How well you keep your customers informed;
- The after-sales service you provide.

Peter Doyle (2001), (23) suggested that to establish an effective delivery system to meet customer requirements, the following criteria should be considered:

- **Availability:** Ideally a company should be able to meet all customer orders from its stock and finished goods.
- **Speed of delivery:** Customers like rapid delivery and some will pay a premium to acquire it.
- **Reliability:** Customers want dependability; they want to know they are going to receive what they have ordered.
- **Lot size:** Customers want to know that the lot size i.e. the number of units that the customer is permitted to buy is available.
- **Convenience:** The more outlets the channel has, the more convenient it is for customers to purchase.

Customers became the focus in the late 1980s and 1990s. Those organisations which paid attention to customers succeeded in achieving their strategic objectives. The slogan for that period was not just to satisfy customers but to delight them.

Suppliers need to ask the following questions in order to serve their customers best:

- What is your value proposition to your customers?
- Why do they do business with you?
- What is it you do better than your competition?

Many organisations initiated various projects to bring about the 'voice of the customer' in their organisations. Among such projects were:

- Customer focus group: A panel of customers is interviewed about the company and their competitors; customers/prospects are invited to discuss a particular topic, for example, on-time deliveries or product design.
- Visits to customers: Taking cross-functional groups from the organisations to visit existing and potential customers.
- Customer councils: Groups of customers who meet regularly to advice the company.
- Questionnaires/postal surveys/ tele-surveys: Questionnaires would be sent out to find out about the quality of the product/service and aspects of service delivery.
- Customer research: Third party companies would be asked to conduct research on customers – finding out them spend, their relationship with the organisation they are dealing with and so on.

Nowadays some organisations have initiated customer 'blogs' to collect information on the products and the quality of customer service.

According to late Peter Drucker, giving customers what they want is nothing but elementary marketing. It is all about getting insight into customer values.

The focus on customer satisfaction has also been highlighted by numerous management writers including Tom Peters, Ohmae and Rosabeth Moss Kanter.

Flows from supply to demand

Economics does not tell much about the nature of suppliers; the subject focuses its attention on the concept of supply and its relation to price and suppliers are presented as entrepreneurs. The types of suppliers such as monopolist, oligopolist or duopolist are dealt with in relation to the types of competition and competitors.

Middlemen

Middlemen existed in the form of wholesalers and distributors. In some businesses and products, they still exist and belong to a marketing network. They were mainly dominant in the first half of the century when large numbers of manufacturers and importers were small organisations. Middlemen provided storage facilities including purchasing. Nowadays many organisations form strategic partnerships with organisations owning transport fleets and warehouses.

Producers have options of dealing with various distribution channels depending on which channel is going to best meet their objectives. Some of the processes involved in making channel choice involve analysing customer service needs and how to provide them effectively; look at constraints and objectives of the channel involved; identify the option for each channel – direct marketing, tele-selling, e-commerce and so on; examine the options from viewpoint of cost, flexibility and control.

In the traditional chain of distribution there can be duplication of the functions. In order to stream line functions to gain control and reduce costs, a single member of the channel co-ordinates or manages the functions and activities in order to increase efficiency. This is known as vertical marketing system. On the other hand, when an organisation buys one or more other organisations at the same stage of distribution this is known as horizontal channel integration. Administrative economies of scale can thus be achieved and specialisation can be increased to achieve efficiency.Vertical and horizontal channel integration provides good examples of the concept of economies of scale in economics.

The concept of supply chain

In order to respond to customers' demand, organisations specialise in sourcing raw materials and then manufacturing them to meet the demand. In many cases manufacturers do not deal directly with the customers or consumers. As a consequence, intermediary organisations have developed to distribute manufactured goods. In case of big businesses, special purchasing organisations have developed to buy products on behalf of these businesses. Thus the concept of supply in practice very much more complicated than it is reflected in Economics.

Traditionally manufacturing, distribution and purchasing organisations acted independently along the supply chain. Over the years these organisations came together to form an integrated chain and this is structure is known as supply chain. Such a chain also incorporates transport of material thus involving logistic operations. The main objective of supply chain is to move goods and services from manufacturers to customers. Supply chain activities involve transformation of raw materials to finished product to meet aggregate demand or market demand.

From a marketing point of view, logistics plays a very important part in addressing marketing mix strategy. Traditional marketing mix has four components, namely, product, price, place and promotion. Place component ensures that the manufactured or finished product is at the right place and the right time to meet demand. It is said that the ultimate aim of any supply chain management system is to reduce inventory but to meet demand 'just in time.'

Since cost of production plays a key role in supply and suppliers are in a business to make profit, supply chain management plays a key role in reducing cost.

Supply involved four types of decisions which economists as well as marketers have to pay attention to. Some marketing gurus have suggested the following four types of decisions:

- **Location decisions:** The geographic location of plants and production facilities. Should the plant be located in Home country or abroad where labour cost and other resources are relatively cheaper than in the home country? Should organisations open or build factories in China or India or in the Eastern European countries to manage cost?

- **Production decisions:** The organisations have to decide what products to produce and which plants to produce in bearing in mind the capacities and the technology required.
- **Inventory decisions:** Inventories exist in every stage of supply chain and the challenge is to manage them effectively to control cost. Decisions also have to be made to create buffers to deal with uncertainty in supply or breakdown in technology.
- **Transportation decisions:** Decisions as to the type of shipments to use to make sure the finished products reach consumers through the organised network of distributors, warehouses and retailers.

In Economics, emphasis is put on costs in dealing with supply. Costs are divided into marginal costs, average costs and total costs. Marginal cost is the cost of producing each additional unit. Average cost is the average of total cost.

Marginal cost is an additional cost of producing an additional unit of a product. It is assumed in Economics that firms want to maximise profits and to do so their marginal cost should equal marginal revenue i.e. an additional revenue gained by selling an additional unit.

In practice, profit maximisation is not the main or the only goal. Firms might want to maximise sales or increase market shares or follow strategies advocated by Ansoff's market. The name of the game is to gain and sustain competitive advantage. Among the strategies they might pursue is to outsource key activities in order to create lean organisational structure.

E-Commerce

E-commerce has developed since the beginning of EDI (Electronic Data Interchange) and there are now a number of diverse applications bringing a variety of benefits such as reducing purchasing cycle times, eliminating administrative errors, increasing buyer productivity, better information management and improving the payment process. Digitisation is transforming boundaries of value chains within the organisation. E-commerce now enables organisations to source certain products and services and resources globally quickly and effectively.

Capabilities of the internet

- The internet facilitates the spread of information.
- It creates a market where buyers and suppliers (demand and supply) come together.
- It facilitates human interaction, thus enabling suppliers to gather valuable information about customers' profile and needs.
- It offers significant marketing opportunity.
- It is used to control and mange inventories effectively.
- It shifts the balance of power from business to consumers.
- It slashes time and costs out of supply chain. It is reported that Eastman Kodak saved over $12 million a year on postage, printing, paper and administrative costs per year by using the internet.
- It provides global reach in marketing. It transforms market place into market space.
- It can facilitate supply on 24/7 basis.
- It is condensing the process of product development and production. Some companies have located product development activities and production processes in different locations worldwide with different time zones which means that products can be developed, produced and marketed in a very short time scale.
- It enables one-to-one marketing and customisation. For example, customers now can design their own car by click of a button.
- It enables the creation of borderless organisation.
- It transforms value chains into value networks.

- It facilitates effective use of Big Data and creation of innovative intelligence.
- It promotes the Internet of Everything offering connectivity of various devices (Things). According to Allied Business Intelligence research and estimate more than 30 billion devices will be wirelessly connected to the Internet of Things by 2020.
- It facilitates cloud computing in that as explained earlier massive amount of data and programmes are being stored and accessed over the internet instead of computer hard drive.

Going as far back as 1998, it was reported in Business Week (24) that by using the Internet and its Intranet, Cisco built a network of partners, making the constellation of suppliers, contract manufacturers and assemblers look like one company to the outside world. Via the company's Intranet, outside contractors directly monitor orders from customers and ship the assembled hardware to buyers later in the day often without Cisco even touching the box. By outsourcing production of 70 per cent of its products, Cisco has quadrupled output without building new plants and has cut the time it takes to get a new product to market by two thirds, to just six months.

When suppliers build their websites they have to address the following questions:

- Is your site fast and user-friendly?
- Does it add value for your customers?
- Is information updated regularly? Continuous improvement is a must for an effective web-site.
- Does it incorporate adequate customer support?
- Is it too complicated?

Designing customer-friendly, easy to use website constitutes one of the key components (place) of market mix.

E-Supply

There are a range of products that can be supplied electronically. This is the concept of e-supply or e-distribution. Groceries and clothes ordered on-line can only be delivered physically to final consumers but there are other products such as books, conference papers, case studies, reports, music and games that can be supplied electronically. The most interesting example at present is the e-supply of music and games and ring tones. Music can be downloaded to MP3 or iPods via computer. Many hotels now secure bookings through various electronic distribution channels.

Using the latest e-business technology, some organisations have managed to reduce processing time and cost, improve business efficiency, improve sales and service quality. These organisations have been able to integrate their electronic distribution strategy with their overall sales and marketing plans.

In formulating e- supply systems organisations now have to increasingly deal with "digital youths" especially in the field of music and entertainment markets.

Customisation

In practice, the concept of supplier is more complex than the one provided in Economics. In marketing sense, suppliers involve manufacturers, distributors and dealers. However, nowadays some businesses like Dell have adopted a business model based on Economics. They become direct suppliers to consumers and customers. Dell, for example, is in business to manufacture and supply products to order. Dell bypasses the dealer channel through which personal computers are sold. They sell directly to consumers thus eliminating costs and risks associated with carrying large inventories of finished goods. Such a business model facilitates building relationship with customers. The distinction between consumers and suppliers become blurred. According to Michael Dell, Boeing, for example has 100,000 Dell PCs and Dell has 30 people that live in Boeing thus looking like Dell being Boeing PC's department. (25)

The marketing strategy of such business assumes different principles compared to manufacturers which have to deal with distributors and agents. This is what customisation is all about. It involves addressing each group of stakeholders including customers to meet their specific needs. This involves empowering customers to design the product and service offering of their choice. This is the concept of one-to-one marketing of customised products. In conventional as well as digital marketing customer involvement and satisfaction play important role. According to Justin Taylor, (26) Managing Director of Graphitas, the platforms we use to engage our audience may change but the marketing fundamentals of engaging them remain exactly the same. He gives the example of printing a name on a bottle of a Coke. It has been done well in order to stimulate emotion and engagement connecting people with the brand. According to him, the Coke example is a textbook example of understanding a brand and more importantly a brand understanding of its audience. Another example one can use is that of Pizza Hut which by creating its app facilitated customers' need of creating their own pizza. The iPhone then enabled the customers to go to their nearest location it is reported that within two weeks, the Pizza Hut app was downloaded 100,000 times and within three months iPhone users ordered $1m worth of pizza.

Customisation in the digital marketing situation is being transformed into personalisation. Marketers keep in touch with customers in a real time situation.

Readers are advised to read *The Economist* August 29, 2015 pp 53-54 the article on '*A brand new game. Marketing in the digital age,*' to look more into the use of social media in marketing.

Chapter Three

Economics of Services

Nature of services

In Economics no distinction is made between goods and services as such. Because most of economic principles were postulated during the period when the economies were dominated by agricultural and manufacturing sectors, the principles are applied to tangible products.

Agricultural activities were categorised as primary sector, manufacturing activities as secondary sector and services associated with both categories of activities were categorised as tertiary sectors. Services were dominated by the activities of the banks in order to finance trade transactions.

According to some reports, Great Britain exported about as much foodstuffs as she imported during 18th century. The 18th century was also the period of steam power and iron and steel. The period from 1760 onwards was categorised as the period of the Industrial Revolution. During this period per capita income rose and the nature of demand changed as well from agricultural products to industrial products. Thus began the industrialisation process and with it was associated labour mobility and the growth of urbanisation facilitated by transport developments.

The beginning of the 20th century saw the demand for services in a form of financial services, health services, leisure and tourism and entertainment. The share of the services as far as Gross Domestic Product (GDP) was concerned was increasing. The structure of the economy was gradually being dominated by the service or tertiary sector and we were entering post-industrialisation stage.

Services gradually became important in the structure of many countries and they began to make significant contribution to the Gross Domestic product and employment.

Writers on marketing focused mainly on marketing of tangible goods. It is not only till very recently the attention turned to applying marketing concepts and principles to marketing services.

Marketing mix – From tangibles to intangibles

Traditionally marketing mix consists of four key ingredients, namely Product, Price, Place and Promotion. These four components are applied mainly to tangible products.

Product. The product manufactured has to meet demand and satisfy consumer's needs. The concept of product, therefore, focuses on what people want to buy rather than what suppliers want to sell.

Products are divided into consumers' products and industrial products. Consumer's products are goods such as food, clothes, cars, and newspapers, DVDs, iPods and so on which are bought directly by consumers. Consumer products can further be divided into necessities and luxury products.

Industrial products are produced for businesses in order to enable them to facilitate production. Examples of industrial goods would be machinery, trucks and Lorries for transport, stationery for business, raw materials and so on. The important distinction between consumer goods and industrial goods depend on for whom the goods are produced and how they are used.

For example, computers can be consumer goods if bought to use them socially as well as industrial goods if bought for business. Kitchen utensils can be produced for consumers as well as for businesses often known as industrial utensils.

In Economics no distinction is made between consumer's goods and industrial goods though distinction is made between necessities and luxury goods as far as consumer goods are concerned.

As we have stated in earlier chapter, according to the theory of demand quantities demanded vary according to price changes. Generally speaking, when price falls quantities demanded increase but when price increases, the quantities demanded decrease. This happens because when the price falls, consumer's real income rises and, therefore, he or she can afford to buy more. However, in some cases consumer may actually buy less when price decreases. These goods in Economics are termed as 'Inferior' goods. These goods such as bread are normally bought by consumers who have very limited income. When price drops, their real income increases hence they make a decision to buy less of that good and instead spend their money on good or better substitutes.

Marketers distinguish between a **product, a product line and a product mix**. A product is a specific item such as a lipstick where as a product line is a group of related products in the same category such as eye shadows or other facial cosmetics. Product mix, on the other hand, consists of different product lines offered by suppliers or produced by manufacturers.

Some manufacturers and suppliers brand their products in order to differentiate them from the products for their competitors. Branding in marketing is very important.

A **brand** is a name, design or symbol that identifies the products of a supplier or a manufacturer. A brand communicates attributes such as speed, quality, (durability), benefits (such as comfort, pleasure) personality (matching the desired self-image of buyers with the brand's image) and values honesty, (integrity).

Companies such as Coca-Cola, McDonalds, Sony, Microsoft, Kodak, Disney, Virgin, have become world leaders through the strength of their brands. Similarly, products such as Kellogg, Nescafe, have become best sellers due to their brands.

Consumers establish a set of beliefs about a particular brand. These beliefs are based on preconceptions, which in turn create expectations. What organisations and marketers have to do is to manage these expectations.

Branding services

Services are **intangible products**. Their attributes are different from tangible products. Services are intangible and they are consumed almost immediately on receiving them. Most service products such as listening to an opera, or a lecture are perishable; they cannot be stored. They are often inseparable from their providers. A singer cannot be separated from his song if one wants to experience 'live' performance. Services can also not be packaged or transported.

Some services such as hotels or restaurants have tangible aspects associated with them. The experience of eating in a restaurant (service) has food and tables and chairs and physical location associated with it. It is suggested if more than 50% of the value of any transaction comes from intangible nature of that product then it should be categorised as service.

The concept of branding has also been applied and is being applied to services. Organisations like McKinsey, Pricewaterhouse-Coopers (PwC), IBM and so on supplying consulting and other services packaged as 'solutions' products. These service providers adopt differentiation strategy to impact upon their existing and potential customers/clients. Differentiation is concerned with *how* the firm competes – in what ways the firm offers uniqueness, e.g. *consistency, reliability status, quality and innovation*. It is the associations which consumers make with the brand that establish an emotional and a rational 'pact' between the supplier and the consumer.

Technological development and automation will play very key part in establishing intense brand relationships with clients, the service consumers.

Product Life Cycle Concept

When products are introduced to the market, over the period they go through various stages of life cycle. These stages are introduction stage, growth stage, maturity stage and decline stage.

Chapter three. Diagram 4. Product Life Cycle.

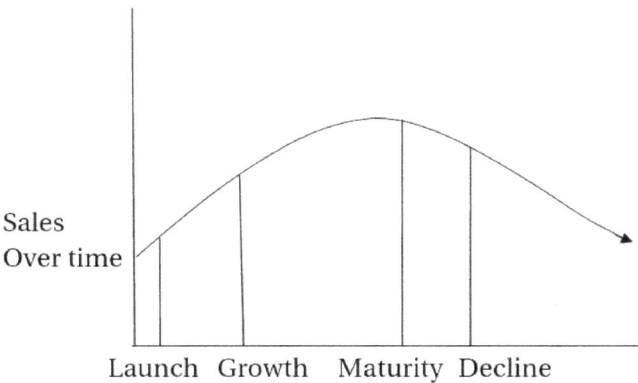

Sales Over time

Launch   Growth   Maturity Decline

At introduction stage, consumers are just being made aware of the product and suppliers invest a lot to promote this product. Once sales increase and promotion of the product is consolidated, the sales begin to rise. This is the growth stage of the product and at this stage supplier will be making profit. Over a period, the maturity stage enters in and the growth in sales begins to slow down. Suppliers make an attempt to promote this product in order to maintain sales growth and they incur heavy marketing costs at this stage. Finally, sales and profit begin to fall and the product enters decline stage.

However, it should be noted that in practice many suppliers do not wait for their products to enter maturity or decline stage. If they adopt continuous improvement strategy, their products will survive for a long time. If you consider razor blades, continuously improvements are being made by different manufacturers in order to retain or even improve their market share. Businesses have to focus on development in technology and use of digital media in order to manage their product life cycles effectively

According to Accenture,

"Innovative digital solutions can reduce costs and add value at every stage of a product's life cycle, within each stage of the value chain and across its entirety. It is essential for businesses to harness the synergies of a fully integrated value chain—one that is based on and supported by digital technologies—so that digitization can truly pave the way for the next industrial revolution." (27)

Communication with businesses and customers happens right throughout the product life cycle. The focus should always be on constant interaction and it is this interaction based on the organisational objectives that deliver business efficiency.

Services do have similar life cycle in spite of their unique characteristics. Suppliers of service have continuously to improve their service in order to retain their customers and the service will only enter maturity and decline stage if suppliers fail to adopt innovative strategy.

Service providers also face intense competition and in many cases such as in consultancy the services offered are similar. They have to create loyalty among their customers and clients and to be careful to see that their reputation does not suffer to scandals and poor service. Arthur Anderson was well-known brand for service provider. The scandals and malpractice contributed to their downfall.

Service providers have to constantly monitor their revenue streams in dealing with different segments of customers they serve. They have to weigh up the costs and revenues associated with different customers over the life time of the service.

According to Lovelock and Wirtz (2007), (28) service organisations should differentiate their offerings in a face of competitive situation. They should be distinctive in the way they present themselves to their targeted customers.

Marketing writers categorise services as **core services, supplementary services** and **enhanced services**. Giving advice on a specific legal issue is providing a core service. How this service is delivered, courteous and expert adviser- relationship with a client – the
way bill is explained and paid – explanation of the documents produced and so on constitute supplementary service. Supplementary
services augment the core product and thus create value to customers. Supplementary services also enhance differentiation. Supplementary services can also be divided into facilitating supplementary services which are required to facilitate the delivery of the service (information, billing, payment) or enhancing supplementary
services (courtesy, creating relationship with customers) which add
an additional value for customers.

In relation to service product life cycle, when core product enters
maturity stage, supplementary services can be used to augment the
core product and stop core product entering into decline stage. To
do that demands creativity and innovation in marketing.

Service providers also have to consider what markets they want
to serve and what services they want to offer. If we take law firms,
for example, some law firms provide an extensive range of legal services to all types of markets while there are other firms who specialise in targeting only so called net worth individuals (private clients-
rich people) to manage their wealth.

According to Robert Johnston (1996), (29) service organisations
strategic focus can be described along two dimensions, namely
market focus and **service focus**. Market focus firm serves few or
many markets, whereas service focus firm offers few or many services.

A **fully focused** service provider offers a limited range of service
to a narrow market segment. A legal firm, for example may decide

to offer only off-shore taxation services to high net worth individuals.

A **market focused** service provider focuses on dealing with a narrow market segment but offers a wide range of services. Taking the same example of a legal firm, it may decide to offer all types of legal services but only to narrow segment of clients.

Service focused service provider may offer a narrow range of service to broad market segments. A legal firm may decide only to offer employee protection rights advice and services to all segments of the market.

Finally, **unfocused service** provider will offer a broad range of services to broad range of market segments. Many public agencies come under this category of service providers.

Price

Price is another key component of marketing mix. It represents the value of a product or service for both the suppliers and customers. For suppliers prices they charge would cover the cost of production plus profit whereas for customers the price they pay represents 'value for money.'

The next chapter will look at how prices are determined in Economics and the role of pricing in marketing.

Place

Place refers to distribution strategy. A supplier has to decide how to get goods to consumers; in other words, it has to consider its distribution strategy. Place component of marketing mix involves transport, warehousing, materials handling and channels of distribution.

Car manufacturers, for example, have a large body of independent dealers in different regions to supply different models of cars manufactured by a specific manufacturer.

Nowadays, place also involves doing business on-line. You can get an insurance quote, for example, on-line and should you decide to take a policy you can order on-line and have policy documents delivered electronically.

In a digital world significant proportion of products and services are purchased on line. There is a combination of seeing theatrical plays on the stage and on TV or on another mobile device such as telephones or i-pads.

Promotion

Promotion involves all forms of marketing communication including, advertising, sponsorships and personal selling.

Promotion should focus on selling benefits not features to consumers. In marketing washing machine, for example, do communicate with potential consumers the benefits of the washing machine rather than highlighting the features of the machine. The machine has x type of design and y rotation is of less importance to consumers than what these features deliver.

A feature is an attribute of a product or service. To determine the benefit, you have to ask **"What's in it for me?"** Benefits are related to consumers' needs and wants.

However, it is easier to highlight benefits in relation to physical goods compared to services as services are what service providers do. Inseparability means that the person performing the service, for example, a lecturer, a singer or a waiter is involved in the service itself and becomes part of the service.

Product, price, place and promotion constitute key components of marketing mix as far as tangible products are concerned but they also apply to marketing services.

However, in addition there are three more components to consider in relation to marketing mix applied to services. They are process, physical evidence and people.

Process

Processes are very important in services since in most cases the customer is directly involved in the processes. It is very important to create systems and design processes in order to deliver high quality service consistently. Badly designed processes result into low productivity, low morale as far as front-line staff are concerned and bad experience for customers.

Marketing experts advise in designing an effective process to deliver core product as well as supplementary product is to adopt flowcharting technique which displays the nature and sequence of the different steps involved in delivering both categories of services to customers. Flowcharting enables in-depth look at the elements involved in augmenting a core product.

Shostack (1992) (30) devised a new tool for creating service process known as **blueprinting.** It is more sophisticated and detailed compared to flowcharting. It highlights the nature of the service and details specifications to which the delivery should conform. In this tool all the key activities involved in creating and delivering the service are identified and the linkages between these activities are then specified.

Blueprinting distinguishes between what customer's experience "front-stage" and the activities of employees and support processes "backstage." Between the two lies what is called *the line of visibility.*

The service system blueprint enables both managers and service staff to see "the big picture," to visualise the entire service system as an integrated whole.

Physical evidence

Physical evidence is about the environment in which the service is offered and consumed. Physical evidence involves corporate logos, corporate colours, the way employees dress and present themselves, cleanliness and so on.

Many writers cite Disney Theme Parks and their impact on customers as good example of the importance of physical environment in enhancing service experience. It serves as message-creating medium and captures customer's attention and enhances their experience. Service environments are also known as *servicecapes.*

The corporate image matters when one is dealing with providing services. Attractive and good quality paper with a clear-produced and well-written letter will help to assure potential and existing customers that they will receive good quality service.

The physical appearance of service provider should be appropriate to the activity, reputation and assumed wealth or income of the organisation.

The appearance of staff is also very important. Many organisations like hotels, supermarkets, hairdressing saloons ask their staff to wear uniforms.

Websites are modern extensions of physical property and to some degree they form part of the service offered to potential customers. The design of the websites is now a distinct professional skill. The site should reflect the corporate image and itself be an evidence of the organisation's ability to communicate effectively with customers. Apart from being user-friendly, it should also focus on providing security both in respect of personal data provided by customers and for payments details provided by customers.

People

In Economics, as far as people are concerned the focus is on wages and productivity. Labour is presented as one of the key traditional factors of production and as all factors of production constitute inputs to producing goods the focus is on the costs of factors of production. For land the cost considered is rent, for capital it is interest, for enterprise it is profit and for it is wages. Costs of inputs play important part in determining price of production.

In marketing, and especially in services marketing, people constitute one of the key components of marketing mix. Services, as we have seen, have distinct characteristics. Because services involve actions or performance, the focus is on people. Appearances, attitude and behaviour of people delivering service be it directly or indirectly influence customer satisfaction.

When we buy physical products, few of us have knowledge or interest in the people who made these products though we would have been influenced by people involved is selling these products to us. When we buy services, we are completely dependent on the attitude, behaviour and performance of people providing service.

Whenever service transactions take place, 'strokes' are exchanged. Strokes may be positive or negative and there are 'give-strokes' (giving) and 'get-strokes' (receiving) situations.

In general, people adopt the following life positions:

'I'm OK, you're OK.'

'I'm OK, you're not OK.'

'I'm not OK, you're OK.'

'I'm not OK, you're not OK.'

Chapter three. Diagram 5. I am ok you are ok.

High   Concern for others   Low

	High Concern for others	Low
High	I'm OK You're OK	I'm OK You're not OK
Concern For self	I'm not OK You're OK	I am not OK. You're not OK
Low		

It is very important to understand the importance of transactional analysis (the way we interact with other people) and to train employees in exchanging transactions and acquiring skills to interact with other people (colleagues, customers, for example) effectively.

When employees are happy at work and given a chance to develop personally and professionally, they will assume 'I'm OK, You're OK mode'. In this mode they will deliver service excellence. If they feel 'I'm not OK, You're Ok' feeling it will stop them from listening to other people (customers).

Training

To sustain delivery of service excellence organisations, need to invest in training their employees in inter-personal relationships and in dealing with customers. Employees need skills required to play their part in fulfilling the expectations of their customers. They have to be trained to deal with difficult, demanding and frustrating customers and clients.

Cole (2003), (31) suggested that the benefits of systematic training include the following:

- The provision of a pool of skilled employees in the organisation.

- The improvement of existing skills. This is important as business situation changes constantly and with these changes come changes in customers' expectations.
- An improvement in job performance with resulting improvement in overall productivity.
- Improved service to customers.
- A greater commitment from employees.

Training can be undertaken internally or externally. Internal training involves working under the supervision of experienced colleague or rotating and enriching jobs to acquire additional skills and to take responsibility for taking decisions.

External training involves taking courses in specific subjects (marketing, customer service, handling complaints, etc.) or attending training provided by external training organisations.

Appearance

Appearance of staff as indicated in physical evidence matter in impacting on customer satisfaction. The appearance of the staff, particularly those in frequent contact with the customers should reflect the activity of the organisation and also give an impression of efficiency. The judgement of customers about the quality of service a company is able to provide is likely to be strongly influenced by their impressions of the people with whom they come into contact during the initial negotiations for a contract.

Empowerment

Empowerment became of the key management buzz words in the early 1990s. Empowerment is about creating situations where workers share power and assume responsibility of making decisions for the benefit of organisations and themselves. Because employees are given more control over how their job is performed, it increases their motivation to undertake tasks in the most effective manner by choosing how to do a task and utilising their talent.

Empowerment is not the same as delegation. Employees assume far more responsibility in empowerment situation and as a consequence they are responsible for their actions. Employees are given freedom to make their own decisions as close to their point of delivery as possible.

Tom Peters in delivering various seminars at the Economist Conferences his book gives the example of a situation when there is absence of empowerment. He has presented one of the following stories in one of his seminars at the Economist Conferences:

"I thought about powerlessness on an icy day, when I ventured into the spectacular new Barney's department store at 61st Street and Madison Avenue on Manhattan's Upper East Side. The weather was far worse than predicted, and I needed something to protect my ears. A watch cap, I thought. To my delight, among Barney's finery, I found one. Oh, did I! It was cashmere. But loath as I am to admit it, I would have paid most anything for a warmth at that moment. (And besides, there aren't many Army-Navy surplus stores in that neck of the woods).
I took the cap, which was missing a price tag, to the register. The clerk said he was sure it cost $45, but he didn't ring it up without tag. In a couple of moments, he caught the eye of a fellow employee, whom he asked to check the price. She retraced my steps to that hat table, found nothing, and came back a moment or two later, claiming she'd contacted a manager to sort things out.
Another three or four minutes passed. Nothing happened. I left.
It's not the shoddy service or the cold ears) that got my goat. It's the missed opportunity. I know it's a cliché, but I didn't present a problem to that clerk, I presented a golden opportunity – Barney's policies, training, recruitment tactics, and frame of mind were what they should have been" (32)

A degree of freedom, involvement and commitment in relation to empowerment depends on the type of organisation and the type of leadership. Empowerment is guaranteed to fail if there is a lack of trust from top management and lack of conviction on the side of employees.

The three most important success factors of empowerment are ability, opportunity and motivation. For empowerment to succeed employees must:

- Be able to make a decision.
- Have an opportunity to make a decision.
- Be wanting to make a decision and take responsibility for their actions.

The following factors contribute to the success of empowerment:

- ✓ There must be information sharing.
- ✓ There should be an inspiring and effective leadership that can facilitate empowerment.
- ✓ There has to be trust on the part of top management and employees.
- ✓ There should be an appropriate training.
- ✓ There should be a tolerant culture.
- ✓ It is important to establish parameters.
- ✓ Managers should assume a role of a coach.
- ✓ The organisation culture should make 'finger-pointing' obsolete. If you come across a problem, you own it.

Many researchers have indicated that employees in an empowered organisation are satisfied. Satisfied employees lead to satisfied customers (I'm OK – You're OK).

Employees as customers
(Internal Marketing)

Employees need to be treated as internal customers. Efforts have to be made to apply the marketing principles internally to employees as well as externally to customers.

Gronroos (1990) (33) identified two separate but integrated elements of internal marketing, namely, **attitude management** and **communications management.** Attitude management is associated with motivating employees to buy into organisation's goals whilst communications management involves providing and managing the information employees need to perform effectively.

If employees are involved in not just delivering but in some situations contributing to formulation of organisation's goals, then when they have to deliver these goals they become more meaningful to them which reinforces their conviction to deliver these goals. In delivering services the conviction enables the establishment of successful relationship with the customers.

The seven components of marketing mix (product/service, price, promotion, place, physical evidence, process and people) as applied to services become the key focus of marketing strategy.

Effective marketing mix delivers satisfied customers which lead to profit and satisfied employees which lead to higher productivity and as a consequence reduction to costs. These are the key elements in Economics.

Professor Philip Kotler (34) was recently asked "where do you think the Four Ps model of marketing, the bedrock of marketing study, stands today?" He stated that the four Ps of marketing is still king.

Most of professional services are also becoming increasingly digitised. There are numerous examples of e- approach provided by health professionals, educational institutions, legal firms and so on.

In article '*The Future of the Professions*', Richard Susskind and Daniel Susskind wrote:

> "*Our main claim is that we are on the brink of a period of fundamental and irreversible change in the way that the expertise of specialists is made available in society. Technology will be the main driver of this change. And, in the long run, we will neither need nor want professionals to work in the way that they did in the twentieth century and before.*" (35)

For more information on digitisation of professional services do read "*Why digitisation is a net opportunity for professional services.*" 17 November, 2015 (36).

Pricing. An important aspect of marketing mix

In Economics, prices are determined by the interaction of demand and supply.

Price and changes in demand and supply

Generally speaking, according to the basic laws of demand and supply, if there is an increase in demand and supply remains the same, price will increase. If there is a decrease in demand, assuming supply remains the same, price will fall. If there is increase in supply assuming demand remains the same, price will fall. If there is decrease in supply and the demand remains the same, there will be an increase in price. Prices will vary till quantities demanded equal quantities supplied. In Economics, this is known as **equilibrium price** (Pe). Diagram 6.

Chapter four. Diagram 6. Interaction of demand, supply and equilibrium price.

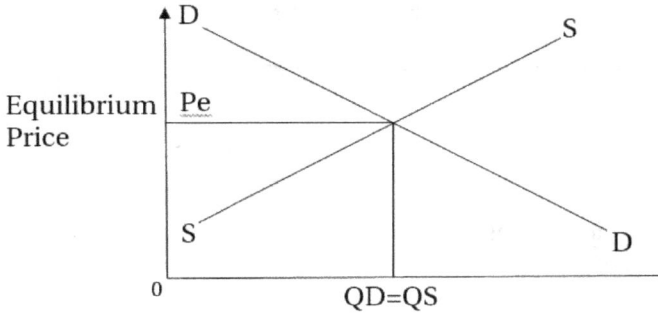

Prices are fixed by interaction of demand and supply. From consumers' side the prices they pay depend on the benefits they get from consuming a particular product or service. The criterion applied is **'is it worth it?'**

From suppliers' side the determining factor is cost. In Economics, costs are divided into **total costs**, **average cost** and **marginal costs**. Total costs relate to costs of using all the factors of production necessary to produce goods or provide service.

Marginal cost is the cost of producing a marginal (additional) unit of a firm's product. Average cost is total cost divided by total output. The table two below shows the relationship between total costs, marginal costs and average costs.

Chapter four. Table 1. Output, total cost, average cost and marginal cost.

Total output	Total costs	Average cost	Marginal cost
Units	£	£	£
1	50	50	50
2	90	45	40
3	120	40	30
4	140	35	20

Marginal cost= 2nd total cost minus first total cost. £50-£0=£50. £90 minus £50= £40. £120-£90= £30. £140 minus £120= £20.

In Economics it is assumed that a firm want to maximise profit. To do so they have to equate total costs with total revenue. Total costs become equal with total revenue when marginal revenue (the revenue derived from selling additional unit) becomes equal to marginal cost. This position in Economics is known as equilibrium of the firm and the entrepreneurs are said to make 'normal profit.' Normal profits in any industry are those profits which are just sufficient to induce the entrepreneur to remain to stay in business.

Price determination

Time plays very important part in price determination. If, for example there is a sudden increase in demand then in a short run it may be difficult for suppliers to increase supply and the result will be consumers have to pay high price. As the time increases suppliers will be able to increase their supply and also high price in the market will attract new suppliers thus increasing supply. The same can be applied if suddenly there is a shortage of supply and the supply decreases. In this situation, assuming demand remains the same, the price will increase. The price determination in a short period will be different from that of medium term or long term.

The other factor in price determination is the nature of competition. In economics, competition is categorised as **perfect competition** and **imperfect competition.** Perfect competition is based on the assumptions that (a) there are large numbers of suppliers so that the action of each supplier in adjusting supply to affect the price becomes insignificant. (b) The products are homogeneous. This means that the products are identical in the eyes of the customers. (c) There are no barriers to entry and exit. As many suppliers can enter the market or leave the market without   incurring costs. (d) There is perfect knowledge on the part of all customers and all suppliers. (e) There are no transport costs to affect prices charged.

As you can see perfect competition is a model rather than a reality. In practice there are imperfections in the market as a result of product or service differentiation on the part of consumers; there is imperfect knowledge; transport costs exist and often there are barriers to entry and exit. In imperfect competition prices are generally higher than it would be in perfect competitive situation and suppliers make, what Economists term 'abnormal profits.'

Imperfect market consists of **monopolistic competition, oligopolistic competition** and **pure monopoly.** In monopolistic competition, there are many buyers and sellers. In most cases goods produced and service provided are similar though not homogeneous. There is product differentiation in a sense that goods and services are branded and suppliers use trade marks to differentiate their products. Because of this, a range of prices occur. Suppliers have an opportunity to augment their products and services in order to create impression of differences in quality. Numerous suppliers and buyers mean that each supplier is less affected by competitors' marketing strategies.

In oligopolistic market there are few suppliers who are highly sensitive to each other organisational and marketing strategies. In oligopoly, without product differentiation, the individual supplier has to consider very carefully what the effects of his or her decisions in relation to price and output would be on competitors. Any move will trigger off a chain of reactions.

Where there is oligopoly with product differentiation, each supplier will have its own segments to focus on. In practice such oligopolists have their own customers who are attached more or less firmly to that supplier. Oligopolistic supplier also makes an added effort to create relationship with customers and come up with ways to build customer loyalty.

Finally, there is a pure monopolist who is the only supplier in the market. In this case prices are handled differently depending on the nature of a monopolist and the segments served. For example, if it is a government monopoly then it might decide to charge different prices according to government guidelines. In reality a private monopolist is also regulated. No one is a complete monopoly because in the end all suppliers must be competing for the limited resources of consumers.

Price discrimination. Price elasticity of demand revisited

In Economics, we have a concept of price elasticity of demand as explained in chapter one. This is defined as the proportionate change in quantity demanded divided by proportionate change in price. As explained in chapter one there is a relationship between elasticity of demand and total revenue gained by suppliers.

If price changes by 10% and as a consequence quantities demanded (sales) change by 20% then we say the commodity in question has elasticity of 2.0 (20/10) – elastic demand. If price changes by 10 % and as a consequence quantities demanded change by 8% then that commodity has the elasticity of 0.8 (inelastic demand).

If demand is inelastic then price increase will result in increase in revenue and price decrease will decrease the revenue. Say current price is £10 and the quantities demanded are 200 units. The total revenue will be £2000. If the price increased to £12 and the quantities demanded fell to 190 units, then the total revenue will increase to £2280. If on the other hand you decrease the price of this commodity to £8 and as a consequence the quantities demanded increase to 220 units, then the total revenue will decrease to £1760.

With elastic demand the tendency will be to increase revenue when price decreases and decrease revenue when price increases. If the price is £10 per unit and the units sold is 200 then total revenues will be £2000. If the price is increased to £12 per unit and the units sold decrease to 150 units, then total revenue will decrease to £1800. If the price of this commodity is reduced to £ 8 per unit and the units sold increase to 280 units, then the total revenue will increase to £2240.

If we take examples of energy and telecom, the demand is elastic during the day time and inelastic at night or during the week-ends. Hence charging higher price during the day time and lower price in the evenings and weekends will increase total revenue. Same applies in relation to travel. Peak periods constitute inelastic demand hence expensive to travel. This practice is known as **price discrimination** in economics — charging different prices for the same services to the same customers at different times or different prices for the same services to different customers (business and domestic).

Some economists have put forward three types of situations where price discrimination can occur even though there is no fundamental difference between the goods offered to each customer.

These situations are:

• Discrimination due to consumers' peculiarities.

These peculiarities relate to lack of knowledge, differences in perception or very insignificant price differential.

• Discrimination based on the nature of the good.

This happens when the good in question is direct service. Dentists, for example, can charge different price to different customers offering the same service as consumers of service would find it difficult to compare the services provided.

- Discrimination because of distances and frontier barriers.

Monopolist will be able to profit from price discrimination if price elasticity of demand of the same good/service is different in each market.

Price fences

Price discrimination is practised by organisations supplying energy for example in order to manage their capacity and enhance their revenue. If the demand for electricity is very high during the daytime, then this put enormous pressure on capacity. In the evening the demand is elastic which eases the burden on capacity. In order to plan for capacity and maximise revenue suppliers practise price discrimination.

Marketers practise revenue or yield management by charging different prices to different market segments. Segments with inelastic demand are charged high prices and the segments with elastic demand or relatively less inelastic demand is charged low prices. Suppliers can predict what the demand level would be at different time and therefore, they can plan capacity utilisation.

Price discrimination is termed as price customisation or price fences in marketing. This is different in price discrimination as explained in Economics in that the prices charged in this case depends on the value the customers put on a service provided. Customers are segmented according to their value propositions. In order to stop high valuers taking advantage of low price, suppliers create fences known as price or **rate fences**. These fences can either be physical in nature or non-physical in nature. Physical fences can be, for example, a room with a view or a room without a view or providing a refreshment facility in a special waiting lounge to high value customers or front tickets in a theatre or speedy check-in at the airport.

Physical fences refer to tangible aspect of the transaction related to different prices.

Non-physical fences include imposing penalty for changing their tickets (low price segments) or non-refundable deposits or a minimum stay in a hotel and so on. Non-physical fences relate to certain buyer characteristics.

Some suppliers have been criticised in creating fences in order to enhance their revenue unfairly. This applies, for example, to some insurance companies who offer low insurance premiums but neglecting to point out 'small print' for exclusions.

Lovelock and Writz (37), the two authorities on Services Marketing, offer the following guidelines in creating price fences:

1. Design prices schedule and fences that clear, logical and fair.
2. Use high published prices and frame fences as discounts.
3. Communicate consumer benefits of revenue management.
4. Use bundling to 'hide' discounts. If a service is bundled into a package the discount is obscured.
5. Take care of loyal customers.
6. Use service recovery such as compensation, alternative arrangements or a substitute service to compensate for overbooking.

Thomas Nagle, Professor in the School of Management, Boston University and a President of Strategic Pricing Group, Boston presented the following seven types of segmentation that have proved effective:

- Segmentation by buyer identification.
- Segmentation by purchase location.
- Segmentation by time of purchase.
- Segmentation by purchase quantity.
- Segmentation by product design.
- Segmentation by product building.
- Segmentation by tie-ins and metering.

"Creating a segmented pricing strategy requires a flash of insight. The manager must recognise different segments and separate them with a pricing policy that is somewhat unique for each product. The manager is most likely to find such insights when he knows where to look." (38)

In his article 'Pricing as Creative Marketing,' Nagle wrote:

"The actual task of pricing falls, however, distinctly and rightly in the domain of marketing because pricing requires more than mere technical expertise. It requires creative judgement and a keen awareness of buyers' motivations." (39)

Marketing mix

In marketing, price constitutes one of the key components of marketing mix. Suppliers fix the price of their products or service on a basis of what is known as cost-plus' approach. They determine the total costs of producing goods or service and add a margin to earn profit.

Costs are categorised as **fixed costs** and **variable costs**. Fixed costs are those costs incurred irrespective of the total output produced. The rent for the premises is, for example, a fixed cost. It does not depend on the volume of service provided or total output produced. Average fixed costs fall as output increases.

Variable costs as the name suggests change according to the units produced or volume of service provided. Cost of raw materials or the salaries of a number of people employed will depend on the demand for goods and services.

Fixed costs are added to variable costs to produce total costs.

Marketers very often use break-even analysis (where total revenue equals total costs) to determine price.

Again, in real business life, there are many complications. Suppliers have to consider the following factors:

- Willingness of consumers to pay the price fixed.
- Close substitutes available in the market.
- The intensity and the nature of competition.
- The prices fixed by competitors.
- The cost of production based on specific location.
- The market strategy of the supplier. Does he want to enlarge the market or penetrate the market or enter new market to increase an overall market share? In many cases suppliers would sacrifice part of the profit in the short run in order to gain bigger market share in the long run.

Activity-based costing

Some organisations use activity-based costing to price their goods and services. This costing system relates directly or indirectly to apportioning costs to all activities a firm has to undertake in order to deliver goods and services to customers.

Organisations undertake various activities which in theory add value at every stage. Porter, M. (1985) (40) presented the concept of **value chain**. According to him, value chain involves firm's infrastructure, human resources, technology, procurement, inbound and outbound logistics, and operations marketing and sales.

Inbound logistics, outbound logistics, marketing, sales and service constitute the firm's primary activities. Procurement, technological development, human resource management and infrastructure constitute support activities.

The focus is on the firm's activities and how value is added at each stage of the value chain. In configuring and analysing a value chain - for example inbound logistics (materials handling, inspection, just-in-time delivery) operations (assembly, testing, processes, plant operations), outbound logistics (order processes, transport), marketing and sales (product pricing, promotions, distribution) – firms stand to gain an insight into their own abilities to satisfy customers.

When a supplier reviews all activities (flowcharting/blueprinting mentioned in earlier chapter) these activities consume resources (material, time, skills etc.) that have to be paid for. Once the costs of the activities have been identified, the cost of each activity is attributed to each product or service to the extent that the product /service uses the activity. The system is very useful in allocating fixed costs to activities in question.

Activity-based costing was introduced because traditional costing system did not facilitate assigning of overhead costs (fixed costs) to products and customers. Activity-Based Costing traces historical costs resources consumed to activities and then through those activities to products or services provided.

Chapter four. Table 2. Example of Activity-Based Costing. Fulfilling customer order.

Activity	% of time spent	cost assigned	activity quantity	cost-driver rate
Process customer Order	60%	£300,000	50,000	£6 per order
Handle customer Inquiries	10%	£500,00	1000	£50 per quantity
Credit Checks	30%	£150,000	2500	£60 per check

Activity-Based Costing system is useful where a firm deal with provision of services.

Pricing in Marketing

According to marketing gurus, marketers have to pay attention to the following pricing strategies:

Market-skimming pricing.

This type of pricing is normally associated with new products. In the initial stage of the product life cycle demand is likely to be less elastic (less price-sensitive) and it will be a unique product in a short term. For example, when Apple introduced iPod it was very unique. The price set was high. Gradually MP3 players came in the market and the price of iPods began to fall. When the price is set high at an early stage of a new product it focuses on a segment that can afford to pay high price. Gradually as price falls, it becomes attractive to other segments in the market.

Also in some cases the supplier sets very high price to test the market. If it does not work, he has a scope to reduce the price.

Penetration pricing

In this case a low price is set in order to penetrate new or existing market. Attracting larger number of buyers means more volume which means reaping economies of scale and reducing average total cost. If demand of the product is inelastic, then charging low price can backfire in that it will adversely impact on total revenue generated.

Optional–product pricing

Some suppliers offer to sell optional or accessory products along with the main products. This is very common when you are purchasing a product on-site. If you are thinking to purchase a camcorder, often there is a link to accessories such as carrier bag or batteries or memory sticks.

If you are buying a car now days the options are heated windows, heated seats, satellite navigator and so on. It is the same if you are buying a computer. If you visit Dell website you have choice of buying a strip-down model and then given a numerous option to increase memory, and other options to enhance the core product.

Captive-product pricing

Some products like printers cannot be used on their own without using cartridges. Suppliers that make products that must be used along the main product are using captive-product pricing. All-in-One printer Lexmark printer costs £40.00 but the cartridges needed to run the printer costs on average about £20.00 each.

Product-bundle pricing

Some suppliers 'bundle' their offer and charge one price. An airline company would sell a ticket to fly plus hire car plus hotel accommodation as 'bundle' product with a composite price.

Loss-leader pricing

Some suppliers, especially some supermarkets deliberately set very low prices (in some cases well below costs) to attract customers to enter the store. These goods are known as **loss leaders** and their main objectives are to attract customers through the door and to undercut small suppliers.

Premium pricing

This happens when suppliers charge very high price in order to attract status-conscious customers. Such customers associate high price with superior quality or they simply want to show off their status or their wealth.

Apple set premium prices for their iPods and iPhones when first introduced.

Psychological pricing

When a supplier wants consumers to respond on an emotional basis rather than rational basis. For example, the laptop priced at £299.99 (not quite £300.00!).

Value pricing

The supplier adopts this type of pricing in order based on external factors such as credit crunch where money becomes tight hence supplier's offers 'value' products to help consumers. Example 'buy one get one free.'

Not-for-profit organisations

So far we have focused on commercial or for profit organisations. The question is doing these economic principles and marketing principles apply to organisations set not to make profit such as public organisations or charities?

Apart from profit motive these principles apply to such organisations. Non-profit organisations such as schools, museums, hospitals, sports centre and so on, according to Weinberg and Lovelock (1978) (41) have four major characteristics. They are:

1. Multiple publics. This means that the organisations have a key stakeholder with their interests and objectives. One Children's Charity recently identified the following as their key stakeholders:
   - Local Authority Social Services Departments.
   - Local Education Authorities.
   - Probation Departments.
   - Schools.
   - Pre-school playgroups.
   - GP Practices.
   - Housing Associations.
   - Police.
   - The church.
   - Health trusts.
   - Home Office.
   - Local MP.
2. Multiple objectives. Non for profit organisations tend to pursue several key objectives simultaneously.
3. They provide mainly services rather than goods.
4. They come under public scrutiny.

Commercial organisations have to make profit but their profit depends on satisfying their customers. Without customers there is no business and no profit. Not-for-profit organisations have to satisfy their customers as well be they patients, students, museum goers or sports members. They have to achieve their organisational objectives efficiently and effectively.

Not-for-profit organisations, therefore, have to pay attention to satisfying consumers, gaining and retaining loyalty, adopting marketing mix strategy and formulating an appropriate marketing communication strategy.

Some marketers adopt **4Cs approach** to marketing mix when dealing with non-profit organisations as opposed to 4Ps. Traditionally 4Ps of marketing mix represent product (quality, quantity, design, differentiation, branding), price (level, policy, margins) place (channels, physical distribution) and promotion (direct and indirect, advertising, exposure, campaigns). Some transform these 4Ps to 4Cs representing customer value (performance, perception, service) cost to customer (cost of ownership, value for money, opportunity cost, time) convenience (accessibility, easiness, time) and communication (two-way, empathy, honesty).

In terms of pricing their services, non-profit organisations have to align their pricing policy with the objectives they want to achieve. According to Kotler (1982) (42), non-profit organisations can adopt four different types of pricing strategies. They are:

1. Surplus maximisation. Some charities organise events to achieve surplus (overcosts) in order to fund the project or project they have planned. To achieve surplus, they have to be good at estimating demand and working out their costs.
2. Usage maximisation. Some organisations like museums want to maximise the total number of visitors to their museum. They might decide not to charge any price or fix very low price.
3. Market Disincentivisation. Very high price is fixed in order to discourage people from buying the product or using the service. Congestion charges in London have been introduced to reduce traffic congestion.
4. Cost-oriented pricing. Prices are set on the basis of costs. Gift shops at Zoo or Museum or National Trust parks may set the price by putting a percentage over their costs mark-up pricing).

Chapter Five

Firms and the Benchmarking

So far we have examined the nature of demand and supply, the differences between goods and services and the way prices are determined in economics and in marketing. In reality the competition is imperfect and in economics emphasis is paid on exploring the nature of competition and the situation of profit maximisation under each competitive situation. The emphasis in economics is on efficiency, whereas in marketing, it is on effectiveness. Efficiency mainly relates to cost consideration and it explained as 'doing things right.' Efficiency is about delivering strategic objectives efficiently –it is described as 'doing right things right.'

In practice businesses do not operate in isolation. They like to find out if their operations, processes and service compare favourably with that of their competitors and some of them strive to deliver best practice. For this comparison some suppliers adopt the practice of benchmarking.

Benchmarking. Best practice approach

Benchmarking is a method used to improve business performance in order to adopt best practice. Over the past three decades benchmarking has become very popular in many organisations. Organisations see benchmarking as systematic process of evaluating companies recognised as industry leaders, to determine business and work processes that represent 'best practice' and establish rational performance goals. Benchmarking practice should be continuous, systematic and that it should involve evaluation and measurement with a view to becoming 'best in class.'

In the late 1970s, Xerox, recognised as being the originator of benchmarking found that the retail price of Canon photocopiers was lower than Xerox's manufacturing costs. They sent a benchmarking team to Japan to compare their performance in a wide range of areas with their Japanese counterparts and returned to undertake the 'step change' needed to catch up. Benchmarking thus developed in Xerox in 1979 and it became company-wide effort in 1981.

According to Coopers & Lybrand's (nowPwC) Survey (1994). (43) which was undertaken when organisations were adopting benchmarking practice, over two thirds of companies in the United Kingdom, the Netherlands and Switzerland, over half of French companies and a third of Spanish companies were using benchmarking techniques then.

Earlier experience of benchmarking was in the manufacturing sector because manufacturing output is tangible and measurable (what gets measured gets managed). Gradually the techniques came to be applied to processes, logistics, financial performance, people management and delivering customer service.

A benchmarking technique can be applied to any organisation be it commercial or not-for-profit to a wide range of functional areas such as finance, production, marketing, people management and so on.

Firms began to form collaborative relationships in order to benchmark against each other. The Rover Group benchmarked against Honda with whom they had established collaborative relationship. Royal Doulton benchmarked against Wedgwood.

Types of benchmarking

Competitive benchmarking: Benchmarking partners in this type of benchmarking are drawn from the same sector. The best example of competitive benchmarking that was used to achieve a quantum leap is given by Michael Hammer (1995) (44) in his book '*Re-engineering the Corporation.*' He gave an example of the Ford Motor Company's efforts to improve its accounts payable operations. Ford benchmarked against Mazda and ended up removing its non-value added activities and thus achieved a reduction in headcount from 500 people to 5 people.

Strategic benchmarking

This type of benchmarking is undertaken when an organisation wants to assess and improve its overall business performance. Organisation undertakes S.W.O.T. (Strengths, Weaknesses, Opportunities and Threats) analysis looking at strengths and weaknesses internally (its core competencies, its processes, its systems, leadership, structure) and opportunities and threats externally (exploring social, technological, economic, environmental and political environment as well as its competitive environment).

It then compares its situation with high performers in its sector to give external reference to the strategic planning process.

Process benchmarking

This type of benchmarking involves comparisons of processes between companies or divisions within the same group. The focus is on improving critical processes and operation. For example, if the Economist Group decides to undertake a comparison of its fulfilment process between the Economist Newspaper and the Economist Intelligence Unit (a member of its group) with a view to improving the process then this would be a process benchmarking.

Sears plc benchmarked against Walmart, Xerox and Marks & Spencer focusing their attention on core delivery processes which develop, select and deliver product to the customer.

Functional benchmarking

In this situation an organisation decides on selecting partners which have good reputation in certain functions such as customer service to benchmark against. The partners do not have to come from the same business sector.

If one chooses to benchmark its customer service in relation to selected partners, this may lead to identifying where performance is below expectations and where improvement is needed.

Internal benchmarking

This involves benchmarking operations, functions or processes within the same organisations. For example, an organisation may benchmark the way payroll administration is done in one business in country 'A' compared to same business in another country 'B' (both companies belong to the same group) or benchmarking certain functions between different business units.

Internal benchmarking has an advantage in that sensitive information can be protected and remains within the organisation.

Some authors recommend using internal benchmarking (a) to establish internal base line (b) to identify performance gaps in various activities (c) to establish best practice and procedure (d) to promote an understanding of the nature of benchmarking and (e) to prepare to undertake external benchmarking.

Product benchmarking

The objective of product benchmarking is to make sure that all new products have superior performance to both the products produced previously by the same organisation and by the competitors. IBM undertook such product benchmarking in 1970s.

International benchmarking

Nowadays, because of globalisation and technological convergence and development, organisations are able to choose their benchmarking partners from further afield. The objective here would be to adopt best practice internationally and to compete effectively in an international arena.

Benchmarking without emotions

Avon Products Inc. decided to benchmark against the model of best practice which they created themselves.

They wanted to review their business with their customers. They used a service quality survey method known as 'servqual' which measured customer expectations and perceptions from which they identified performance gaps.

They grouped together into regional teams in order to identify 'best practice.' The benchmarking was done against an 'ideal; service unit' which enabled everyone to work towards a goal without the emotions of feeling unfairly compared.

How to benchmark

1. Identify what is you want to benchmark and why. Ask your customers, suppliers or partner who they rate as best providers of service and why.
2. Identify the partners you would like to benchmark against.
3. Identify the key performance indicators to measure.
4. Visit the best practice organisations and measure your performance against theirs.
5. Identify the gaps and decide how to fill them.
6. Prepare implementation plan. Decide who is to do what and when to improve the situation.
7. Monitor results and take corrective actions, if necessary.

Sources of information

A question is often asked as to where one can find information on best practice.

Information about other organisations can be obtained from numerous sources. Following are some of the sources of information available to those organisations which want to benchmark:

- Annual reports.
- Press reports.
- Customer's feedback.
- Information from suppliers, distributors, sales people and partners.
- Market research reports.
- Trade associations.
- Case studies.
- Books.
- Competitors' advertising.
- Former employees.
- Benchmarking clubs.
- Site visits.
- Conferences.
- Government publications.
- Industry experts.
- Consultancy reports.
- Information from quality award winners.
- Digital sources.
- Aspects of Big Data.

Advantages of benchmarking

Benchmarking provides the following advantages:

- It provides direction and impetus for improvement and organisational change.

- It makes one look inside and outside organisation.
- It provides one with information that can be turned into knowledge.
- It involves staff in generating ideas to bring about required improvements.
- It promotes competitive awareness.
- It provides an opportunity to collaborate.
- It challenges the status quo.
- It enables organisations to review their core competencies.

Caution!

Benchmarking is about adopting and adapting the best practice. It is not about simply copying the best practice.

Continuous improvement

Benchmarking is associated with continuous improvement. Continuous improvement is linked with total quality management TQM). Quality gurus like Joseph Juran, Edwards Deming and Philip Crosby have advocated adopting total quality improvement initiatives.

TQM is concerned with continuous improvement in performance aimed at delighting customers. It involves achieving improvements of the quality of products and service for the customers. The word 'total' is designed to send the message that it is all embracing programme involving all processes, all people and all levels of management.

Juran set up ten steps to quality improvement. They are:

1. Build awareness of the need for quality and an opportunity for improvement.
2. Set goals for improvement.
3. Organise to achieve goals.

4. Provide training.
5. Carry out projects to solve problems.
6. Report progress.
7. Give recognition.
8. Communicate results.
9. Keep score.
10. Maintain momentum.

W. Edwards Deming was another well-known guru on quality. He presented the following 14 points for management (45):

1. Create constancy for the purpose for improvement of products and service. Allocate resources to provide long-term needs with a view to becoming competitive.
2. Adopt the new philosophy. We are in a new economic age. We can no longer live with mistakes and defects. Western management must waken to the challenge, must learn their responsibilities and take on leadership for change.
3. Eliminate dependence on mass inspection. Quality must be built into the product. Quality must be the foundation on which the organisation is based.
4. Eliminate awarding business based on price alone. Instead minimise total cost. Move toward a single supplier for any one item, on a long-term relationship of loyalty and trust.
5. Improve constantly and permanently the system of production and service, to improve quality and productivity and thus constantly decreasing costs. What is good enough for today is not good enough for tomorrow.
6. Institute training on the job.
7. Institute leadership. The aim of supervision would be to help people and machines do a better job. Supervision of management is in need of overhaul, as well as supervision of production workers.
8. Drive out fear. Create a climate in which every one may work effectively for the company.
9. Break down barriers between departments. People in research, design, sales and production must work as a team to tackle problems encountered with the product or service.
10. Eliminate slogans and exhortations and targets for the workforce asking for zero defects and new levels of productivity. Such exhortations only create adversarial relationships, as the bulk of the causes of low quality and low productivity belong to the system and thus lie beyond the power of the workforce.
11. Eliminate work standards (quotas). Eliminate management by numbers and numerical goals.

12. Eliminate barriers to pride of workmanship. This implies, inter alia, abolishment of the annual or merit rating and of management by objectives. The responsibility of supervisors must be changed from sheer numbers to quality.
13. Institute a vigorous programme of education and self-improvement. Workers should be educated to use tools and techniques of quality as well as develop new methods of working in teams.
14. Take action to accomplish transformation. The transformation is everybody's job.

These 14 points taken together assume holistic approach to quality management.

In the 1960s emerged another quality guru in Philip Crosby. His quality improvement process is based on the following 'absolutes.'

- Quality means conformance to requirement, not goodness.
- Quality is achieved through not appraisal.
- The performance standard is 'zero defects.'

In November 1989, Tom Peters articulated the following six steps to quality in his one of the presentations at the Economist Conferences seminar platform:

Step one: Conformance to specification.

Step two: Ask whose specifications.

Step three: Move beyond the envelope called specification and add perception.

Step four: Getting everybody out in front of the customers.

Step five: Work on a project with a customer.

Step six: Remove internal barriers and external borders.

He also said that it was impossible to progress very far down the road towards true customer satisfaction in quality improvements unless the orientation of the organisation is completely changed.

Most of the quality initiatives have been focussed on tangible products. Services, because of its nature, have to have different focus in relation to quality. Gronroos (2000) (46) distinguishes between functional quality and technical quality. The process of service delivery is functional quality and actual output or outcome of service is technical quality. Customers compare their perceptions of service delivery and its outcome to what they expect. '**What customers perceive; they expect to receive.**'

Zeithaml, Berry and Parasuraman (1990) (47) have suggested that service quality is judged by customers along the following criteria:

- Tangibles (appearance of physical elements).
- Reliability (dependable, accurate performance).
- Responsiveness (promptness and helpfulness).
- Assurance (competence, courtesy, credibility and security).
- Empathy (easy access, good communication, and customer understanding).

These days most customers buy products and services on-line. To keep up with this modern trend Parasuraman, Zeithaml and Malhotra (2005) (48) presented the following criteria to assess service quality:

- Efficiency (i.e. ease of navigation, transactions can be completed quickly and the website loads quickly).
- System availability (I.e. the site is always available. It launches right away and it is stable and does not crash).
- Fulfilment (I.e. orders are delivered as promised and offerings are described truthfully).
- Privacy (there is protection of information provided).

In some cases, customer perception of service quality is based on reputation, professionalism and outcome. It is impossible to receive some service in advance. For example, if the author has a pain in his back he might decide to go to chiropractor based on reputation and recommendation (word-of-mouth). His satisfaction would depend on whether the outcome was satisfactory. Outcome may depend on few days or few weeks.

Process re-engineering

In the beginning of 1990s, benchmarking was also used to re-engineer business processes in order to eliminate activities that do not add value to customers. Michael Hammer and Jim Champy's book '*Re-engineering the Corporation*' became the best seller around the world when it was published in 1995.

The focus of re-engineering is on processes. A process is defined as a set of linked activities that take an input and transforms it to create an output. In an organisation, processes are categorised as 'core' processes and 'support' processes. A core processes create value by the capabilities it gives an organisation Support processes are designed to facilitate operations of core processes.

There are many activities incorporated in the processes that have entered into business over time. Some of these processes do not add value as such but are there because they have always been there and no one has made an attempt to evaluate their contribution.

Business process re-engineering advocates revolutionary approach in bringing about a change which is radical and dramatic in nature. It means throwing away all the rule books and procedural manuals and discarding fundamental assumptions. Organisations which have re-engineered their processes have made dramatic gains. Following are some of the examples of the companies which have achieved dramatic improvements as a result of re-engineering:

- Continental Canada Insurance embarked upon a re-engineering project which took fifteen months. Personal Automobile Insurance outperformed the industry average for profitability by 30% twelve underwriters now do the work of 60 and 120 agents now service a more profitable base of service than 700 did previously.

- Bell Atlantic achieved a five-fold reduction in cycle time as far as customer services are concerned and the labour costs decreased from $88million to $6 million.
- Hall mark cards reduced the new product development cycle from between two and three years to one year.
- National Health Service trust in the UK has cut the cycle time from twelve weeks to less than a day. The trust wanted to reduce time taken for an out-patient clinic to produce diagnostics to cut down administration costs and to increase the satisfaction of patients and staff involved.
- Texas Instruments reduced process cycle time by well over 50%.

Re-engineering processes impact dramatically on reducing costs and improving service delivery. Processes are understood from the perspective of customers rather than from production perspective. It promotes provocative culture – questioning everything an organisation does and seeking innovative ways of doing work. Furthermore, it aligns core processes to business strategy.

In some organisations re-engineering is focused on specific processes, for example process of issuing contracts in terms of tendering or logistics process. This is known as process re-engineering. When the focus shifts to all the processes of the organisation then the outcome of re-engineering is corporate transformation.

Critical success factors of business process re-engineering:

1. There should be a desire to change status quo.
2. There has to be trust, motivation and understanding of what is needed to be done.
3. Top management must give their total involvement.
4. Employees have to be trained and empowered.
5. Organisational structure has to be flexible and responsive to customer needs.
6. Organisational culture has to be supportive of re-engineering initiative. There has to be no blame culture and mentality of 'getting it right first time.'
7. Traditional assumptions have to be challenged.

8. There has to be considerable taken in planning and implementation.
9. The action plan has to be very clear of the objectives to be
   achieved and who is doing what and when.
10. Appropriate performance indicators have to be agreed and put
    in place.

Why have some re-engineering initiatives failed?

The following are the factors which have contributed failures in
practice:

- Lack of clear understanding of what is involved.
- Lack of resources.
- Lack of leadership support.
- Lack of skills and training.
- Poor and ineffective teamwork.
- Poor communication.
- Focus on processes that were too narrowly defined.
- Resistance from various stakeholders.
- Existence of silo attitude.
- Unreasonable expectations.

Jim Rosenthal and Judy Wade (1993) (49) highlighted the following 'Five keys to successful redesign' and 'Four ways to fail.'

1. Set an aggressive re-engineering target. The target must span the
   entire business to ensure sufficient breath.
2. Commit 20 to 50% of the chief executive's time to the project.
3. Conduct a comprehensive review of customer needs, economic
   leverage points, and market trends. For example, customer in-
   terviews and visits, competitor benchmarking, analysis of best
   practices in other industries and economic modelling of the
   business.

4. Assign an additional senior executive to be responsible for implementation.
5. Conduct a comprehensive pilot of the new design.

......and Four ways to fail:

1. Assign average performance. Companies tend to go for average performers because high performers are needed elsewhere in business.
2. Measure only the plan. Plans are followed through with comprehensive measurement system.
3. Settle for the status quo. Companies are not brave enough or lack conviction to adopt innovative approaches.
4. Overlook communication. There is a lack of comprehensive communication strategy.

Use of value chain

Organisation which desire to re-engineer their processes in order to become customer-centric and compete effectively can focus on their value chain. We have already explained the generic categories of activities (primary activities and support activities) involved in the value chain. In theory, value is added at each stage of the value chain.

Use value chain model to analyse activities involved in each stage. Analyse activities and eliminate those activities that do not value to a business in terms of enhancing customer satisfaction and profitability. In a case of not-for-profit organisations the focus should be on activities that add value to delivering services effectively.

Understanding change initiative

Re-engineering, like total quality management or benchmarking brings about change. Change has to be managed very effectively in order to achieve outcomes desired. There are forces such as competition, new leadership, alliances and so on that prompt change and then there are other forces such as employees' attitude to change, corporate culture, lack of resources and leadership that resist change.

Kurt Lewin (1951) (50) identified three critical phases in the implementation of change programme. There are three phases involved, namely, **Unfreezing phase, Changing phase** and **Refreezing phase.**

Unfreezing Phase: At this stage all employees should be prepared for a change. Communicate openly and honestly the need for a change and how individuals and organisations would benefit from this stage. Examine all forces that going to be obstacles to change and focus upon eliminating these obstacles. Get employees to 'buy in' in your change programme.

Changing phase. Start implementing the plan prepared to bring about desired change. Action plan should be very clear as to the objectives to be achieved and who is to do what and when.

Refreezing phase. This is monitoring stage and taking corrective action to keep change programme on track. At this stage the newly acquired behaviour comes to be integrated as patterned behaviour into individual's personality. It is important to monitor this behaviour continuously to see that it does not extinguish over time or that it creates 'burnt out' syndrome.

In this chapter the focus has been on benchmarking, total quality and business re-engineering. These are not management fads but ways to focus on micro-economic aspects of the firm. The firm, in order to be competitive and in order to achieve its objectives cannot remain static. The business world is changing dramatically –it is said that the only constant thing in business is change. We have to assume that firms desire to survive in business; that they have set strategic objectives whatever they may be; that they want to achieve these efficiently and effectively. For these assumptions to materialise the firm has to be a dynamic entity. It constantly has to review its internal competencies in order to meet the challenges of changes taking place externally. If they do not, then they will not achieve what strategist call 'strategic fit' and in time they will drift away. This is what economics of the firm is all about.

Marketers need to come up with ways to enable firm to achieve their objectives. They have to focus on customers and enable the firm not only to gain but to sustain competitive advantage.

The world of digital marketing demands changes internally within the organisation as well externally in dealing with changing customer relationships. The way marketers communicate with customers becomes the focus point of change.

According to David Cooperstein (2012), in his writing on *'Marketing Change Management – Like it or Not, You Have to Figure it out,'* he wrote:

> *"It's clear to me that most of the CMOs and senior marketers I speak to **want** to change and adapt. But they have a tough time understanding **how** to change. The ability to implement process changes and calculate careful organizational impacts will differentiate those CMOs that say they want to change from those that know how to make change happen. As any IT or functional exec who has been through change management would tell marketers, technology does not solve for bad process, it just makes the problem more obvious."* (51)

Modern literature on benchmarking

Numerous articles have been written on the process and benefits of benchmarking. In 2008 ICAEW a professional membership organisation that develops, promotes supports chartered accounts worldwide published information in 2008 on *'10 ways to benchmark your business'* (52). These relate to focussing on business drivers, who to benchmark against, assessing the efficiency of your processes, analysing your location of resources, weighing your costs against industry norms, calculating sales per employee, working out your profit margins, measuring your customer service standards, and obtaining benchmarking information without an external benchmarking partner.

In an excellent report Management Trends and Tools 2013 published by Bain & Company (53), benchmarking is listed as one of the tools that could help organisations managing their businesses in changing economic climate. What to benchmark and which organisations to choose in relation to benchmarking depend on your strategic objectives. Organisations benchmark in relation to achieving best marking related to race and gender, recruitment, diversity policies, customer satisfaction and so on. There also very interesting publication which came out in 2012 which reviews the latest international data benchmarking UK economic performance against its major competitors (54).

Apart from various organisations and professional bodies and Institutes, undertaking benchmarking in order to improve their operations, processes and culture, benchmarking is also conducted at state level. Benchmarking has been done at **e-Government** level in terms of e-Government use of information and communication technologies. Richard Heeks (2006) (55) produced a paper which provides a useful insight into the nature of benchmarking incorporating internal and external perspectives of eGovernment. The other interesting and useful report on eGovernment benchmarking is that prepared by Capgemini, IDC, Sogeti and Politicnico di Milano in 2015 (56) for the European Commission DG Communications Networks, Content and Technology. This study examines the challenges facing some European countries within the context of on digital single market in providing effective and innovative solutions to their practices, attitude and culture.

Overall Benchmarking is geared to deliver Best Practice for organisations which have to compete intensively in the changing business market. The focus of attention generally is on economic criteria including turnover, profit, marketing spends, client types and sectors. In this situation there is a key integration between Economics and Marketing.

In the article "*Future Benchmarking – an innovation tool for creating growth from uncertainty*", Pantea (2015) draws our attention in relation to assumptions underlining future benchmarking. The writer stated:

> "*.... a new set of assumptions is required to guide the benchmarking activity:*
> - *Virtually all industries are undergoing rapid structural change due to continuous emergence of disruptive technology platforms as well as changing geopolitical and economic forces.*
> - *Best practices currently used were shaped in an era of greater stability.*
> - *Any tools and best practices today need to be responsive and adaptable to rapid change.*
> - *New business models constantly disrupt established markets.*
> - *Classic strategy planning is not working anymore, strategy today is a responsive and fluid discipline, which has to identify risks and opportunities and make difficult choices more frequently.*
> - *Success is as much about choosing not to do something, as it is about doing something that was unimaginable before.*"
> (57)

These assumptions enable embracing uncertainty in a changing business world.

Chapter Six

Mergers, Acquisitions and Alliances

Nature of mergers, acquisitions and alliances

In economics, there are basically two types of competition, namely, **perfect competition** and an **imperfect competition**. Perfect competition is unattainable in reality because there are numerous imperfections in the market that create imperfect competition. These imperfections take different forms such as lack of knowledge of prices as far as consumers are concerned, transport costs, few suppliers in the market, various barriers to entry such as massive development costs, complexity of technology, various uses of digital media and platforms, ownership of resources, or trademarks, and so on.

Many firms in a competitive situation deploy various strategies to enlarge, penetrate or capture new markets. Some acquire sources of raw materials or distribution channels in order to consolidate their competitive position and survive in business whereas other acquire new businesses in order to diversify and spread risks.

A merger takes place when two companies combine to form a new company. **An acquisition** occurs when one company purchases another company to form a new company.

Marketing planning plays a key role where mergers and acquisitions involve branded products and services. Prior to planning any merger significant work has to be done in relation to examine the advantages of taking on brands from a merged organisation and what research needs to be taken in preparing strong argument for mergers and acquisitions.

Merger takes place when one firm decides to merge with another firm in order to safeguard its supply or raw materials or to gain control of distribution channels or to dominate the market. There are three types of mergers. They are **horizontal mergers** in which firms in the same industry combine, **vertical mergers** and **conglomerate mergers**. An example of horizontal merger would be the coming together of Exxon and Mobil in 1998 or 2002 merger of Hewlett-Packard and Compaq Computer or Heinz and Kraft merger in 2015.

There are laws in existence in the USA and in Europe to restrict such mergers if they are likely to reduce competition. Mergers taking place in a moderately concentrated or highly concentrated industry are normally challenged. Concentration is concerned with control of market share.

The other type of mergers is known as vertical mergers in which two firms at different stages of the production process come together. The example of vertical merger would be the coming together of Merck, a pharmaceutical manufacturer and Medco, a pharmaceutical distributor in 1993.

When a manufacturing firm merges with a firm supplying raw material to that firm then backward integration and when a manufacturing firm merges with a firm which is its distributor of the products then this is known as forward integration. Vertical integration, according to some economists play key role in reducing costs. On the other hand, there are some economists who argue that mergers necessarily require coordination and such coordination increase administrative costs. Even for vertical mergers the government may restrict such mergers if they are deemed to restrict competition.

The third type is known as conglomerate mergers. In this case firms in unrelated businesses combine to form what is known as Conglomerate Corporation. Such mergers facilitate concentration of assets. Such concentration of assets does not necessarily bring about concentration of market power in individual industries. The example of conglomerate merger would be Daimler Benz's acquisition in sectors such as the aerospace industry.

Mergers, competition and market dominance

Mergers are regulated in some countries, for example, in the USA, and Europe. In the USA, competition law is known as antitrust law. The Antitrust Division of the Department of Justice and the Federal Trade Commission focus on unreasonable monopolistic practices. These practices include agreements prohibiting free trading, price fixing by cartels, banning behaviour that lead to gaining dominant market position, and supervising the mergers and acquisitions of large corporations. In the early years in the US, a rule of reason was used to judge firms' actions. Unreasonable restraints of trade were considered illegal. The courts then adopted per se rule judging firms adopting monopolistic tactics as illegal. In the 1980s and through Regan and Bush administrations, the courts returned to using a rule of reason but based on a looser interpretation than before.

The 1990s witnessed the most intense period of mergers and acquisitions, particularly in the USA. The merger waves also impacted Europe as Europe in the mid-1990s experienced large number of cross-border deals within Europe

Transatlantic deals also started to take place in the late 1990s. Considering the present situation, mergers and acquisitions slowed down during the early period of 2000 and more specifically during the period of financial crisis in the early 2000. However, looking at 2014 and 2015situations, there have been numerous mergers and acquisitions. Some experts have put forward the view that currently low inflation, deflation and low interest rates are pushing organisations to merge. In 2016 experts and business analysts are also predicting to see huge volumes of mergers and acquisitions.

European law and mergers

Under EU rules businesses are not allowed to merge if that would put them in a position to control the market. Larger companies that do a lot of business in the EU cannot merge without prior approval from the European Commission —even if they are based outside the EU (the merger regulation).

Firms proposing to merge have to get authorisation from the relevant government authority. If they go ahead without authorisation, they could be asked to de-merge if the authority find that such a move would lessen competition. Merger control is about predicting what the market will be like and making a judgement accordingly.

Under the EC law, a concentration exists when a *"...change of control on a lasting basis results from (a) the merger of two or more previously independent undertakings... (b) The acquisition...if direct or indirect control of the whole or parts of one or more other undertakings."* (Art. 3(1), Regulation 139/2004, the **European Community Merger Regulation**).

The main objective of merger regulation is to stop merged firm abusing their dominant market position. In certain circumstances as in the case of a firm going out of business if it does not merge or where there is a good technical and economic progress argument, mergers are permitted. In some cases, mergers are approved under certain conditions such as they may be asked to sell part of the combined business or to license technology to another market player.

Some Examples of mergers examined by the European Commission. (58)

Pharmaceutical sector

Mergers of Sanofi/Sythelabo and Pfizer/Pharmacia were notified to the European Commission. "The European Commission concluded that both mergers could have an adverse impact on competition, limiting the choice of certain drugs available to patients. In both cases, the parties proposed transferring some of their products to competitors, which the European Commission agreed would restore competition in the markets and so protect the interests of the patients..."

Consumer goods/food sector

Merger between Unilever and Bestfoods was intended to reduce competition in the markets for instant soups, pasta sauces, jams and other food products in almost all EU Member States. The parties proposed the sale of an estimated Euro 1 billion of their business to competitors and this allowed the European Commission to give conditional clearance to the merger.

French petroleum companies

The merger of TotalFina and Elf Acqutaine was considered to have led to being a leading supplier of liquid petroleum gas and the consequence of such dominance would lead to higher prices. Total-Fina/Elf Acquitaine proposed the sale of large proportion of their operations to competitors and the merger was given conditional clearance.

Globalisation has facilitated cross-border mergers and acquisitions. All such mergers and acquisition come under the scrutiny of relevant competition authorities.

Other examples of mergers and acquisitions:

- In 1992, the Hong Kong and Shanghai Banking Corporation (HSBC) took over Midland Bank Plc to create the second largest non-Japanese bank in the world and the largest in the UK.
- Guiness and Grand Metropolitan merged to create a drinks group called Diageo.
- The Italian phone company Stet bought 25% of Mobilkom, Austria, 49% of Telecom, Serbia and 60% of Retevision.

- Lufthansa formed Star Alliance with SAS, United Airlines, Air Canada and Thai Airways.
- Anglo-Dutch Publisher Reed Elsvier's $8.8 billion stock swap over was agreed with German-Dutch rival Wolters Kluwer.
- British gas acquired 1 61% stake in India's Gujarat gas Co.
- Coopers and Lybrand merged with Price Waterhouse to form Pricewaterhouse Cooper (PwC).
- Worldcom's snatched MCI from the grasp of British telecommunications for $37 billion.
- Daimler-Benz merged with Chrysler.
- British petroleum announced a $30.3 billion takeover of Amoco of the USA.
- The Commission has approved the acquisition of sole control of Nyrstar of Belgium by Refigure of the Netherlands in 2015.
- Commission approves Etihad's acquisition of joint control over Alitalia in 2014.
- Commission approves the acquisition of Skype by Microsoft in 2011.
- Tata Steel purchased Corus in 2007.
- Microsoft acquired Skype.
- Dell acquired EMC in 2015.
- BT acquired EE, the UK's largest mobile group.
- There has been a merger of Facebook and WhatsApp.
- In 2015 the European Commission cleared the proposed acquisition of Aer Lingus by International Consolidated Airlines Group (IAG) under the EU Merger Regulation.

Which mergers are examined by European Commission?

"If the annual turnover of the combined businesses exceeds specified thresholds in terms of global and European sales, the

proposed merger must be notified to the European Commission, which must examine it. Below these thresholds, the national competition authorities in the EU Member States may review the merger. These rules apply to all mergers no matter where in the world the merging companies have their registered office, headquarters, activities or production facilities. This is so because even mergers between companies based outside the European Union may affect markets in the EU if the companies do business in the EU. The European Commission may also examine mergers which are referred to it from the national competition authorities of the EU Member States. This may take place on the basis of a request by the merging companies or based on a request by the national competition authority of an EU Member State. Under certain circumstances, the European Commission may also refer a case to the national competition authority of an EU Member State" (59).

Europe is following USA in relation to formation of mergers and acquisitions. Experts are predicting most of the mergers and acquisitions will be in the area of technology and media and telecommunications and pharmaceuticals.

Market conditions aside, legislation and tax are playing a key role. Jonathan Dunn says: "In general terms, the UK provides a highly stable legal, fiscal and political environment in which to do business. The UK also displays none of the protectionism that can be seen in other developed economies, in stark contrast with France, where both GE and Siemens encountered difficulties in their attempts to acquire Alstom in 2014." (60)

Mergers and acquisition
in the service sector

The European banking sector has experienced a dramatic increase in the field of mergers and acquisitions A report issued by European Central Bank (2000), found that by the late 1990s the total number of mergers and acquisitions within European banking had grown from 326 in 1995 to 497 in 1999. According to European Central bank 2004 Report, from 2000 to 2004, cross border mergers and acquisitions accounted for the all banking mergers and acquisitions in the Euro zone.

Banks have become very acquisitive. The pace of mergers and acquisitions in banking is accelerating not only in the USA but also in Europe and Asia. Recently Spain's Banco Santander Central Hispano acquired Abbey national in the UK. Banking mergers enable banks to expand their retail franchise and offer new products to reach new customers.

Mega mergers also take place within the country. In the USA, domestic mega-mergers include the merger between Bank of America with FleetBoston and J. P. Morgan Chase with Bank One.

Acquisitions

Acquisitions are takeover of one firm by another firm. Firm 'A' may negotiate with firm 'B' to take over its business. The buyer or the firm intends to take over buys the shares of the target company and by getting majority of the shares they gain control of that company. In some cases, acquisitions become hostile. A target firm will resist the takeover.

The Economist Intelligence Report on 'Making acquisitions work,' classify acquirers into (1) the carnivores (b) the dairy farmers (c) the vegetarians (d) the white hunters (e) the gentlemen shooters and (f) the cross-breeders.

The carnivores acquire businesses in order to add synergies to the main business. *"They have rigorous objectives and stick to them. They integrate, make changes and get rid of the bits (and the people) they do not want."*

They cite corporations like Nestle, Unilever, Electrolux and General Electric as the examples of the carnivorous.

The dairy farmers also have clear objectives. *"They increase shareholder value by increasing the value of the company and milking it at the same time. They do not as a rule interfere in the running of their acquisitions, except for insistence on the proper financial disciplines. They do whatever is necessary to nurture the herd, selling off unsuitable parts from time to time and replacing them with healthier ones."*

They cite Hanson, as an example as the dairy farmers.

The vegetarians have less clear objectives. *"Indeed, it is often difficult to detect a strategic or operational reason for their purchases, which tend to be opportunistic although they may be represented as part of repositioning or diversification exercise."*

The examples of the vegetarian include Sony and Matushita's entry into Holywood.

The white hunters are termed as professional acquirers and they do seem to lack industrial or commercial logic. *"The acquirers claim to force lazy management to make underused or undervalued assets work harder or get rid of them."*

The examples cited include WPP takeover of JWT.

The gentleman shooters tend to make one big acquisition at a time. *"They are usually buying for good strategic reasons, and therefore wish to integrate their purchases. They have frequently researched the field and screened a number of possible candidates for acquisition"* (61).

The cross-breeders are a new kind of Eurocompany. These acquirers create trans-European alliances with no discernible national identity. The examples cited include Asea of Sweden and Brown Bovery of Switzerland in heavy electrical equipment; Reed (UK) and Elsevier (Netherlands) in publishing.

Acquisitions are often paid in cash, the acquiring company's stock or a combination of both. In some cases, acquisitions are financed by debt. This is known as leveraged buyouts and in practice, the debt is often moved down onto the balance sheet of the acquired company.

The reasons why mergers and acquisitions take place are as follows:

- To create synergy. It is often expressed as 2+2=5. That is, as the equation shows, the combination of two firms will yield a more valuable entity than the value of the sum of the two firms if they were to stay independent: Value (A + B) > Value (A) + Value (B).
- To increase market share.
- Achieve economies of scale. Economies can be achieved in streamlining management or in purchasing and so on.
- To diversify business.
- To acquire new technology or knowledge.
- Empire-building.
- Reducing tax exposure. In some countries the firms pay less tax if they use cash to acquire assets than if it has cash in hand.

Mergers and acquisitions were mainly being talked and written about with reference to deals in the USA and Europe. But now countries like India is also involved in mergers and acquisitions.

The following is an extract from The Hindu Business Line:

"India is emerging a vibrant player in the world of mergers and acquisitions (M&A). Not long ago, Mr Lakshmi Mittal acquired Arcelor, and had Tata Steel's bid for the Corus group of the UK gone through, it would have made the company the world's fifth largest producer. Tata Group companies and many in the information technology, pharmaceutical and banking sectors have made a host of other acquisitions. Could anybody have imagined such a showing by Indian entrepreneurs even a few years ago?" (62)

In 2015 most of mergers and acquisitions have been in pharmaceutical, healthcare and cable industries.

Strategic alliances

Apart from merger and acquisitions, firms also now get together to form alliances for a variety of reasons. Some experts say that strategic alliances are no longer a strategic option but a necessity in many markets and industries.

A strategic alliance comes into existence whenever two or more independent firms collaborate in the development, manufacture or sale of products or services. Strategic alliances take many forms; they include licensing agreements, marketing agreements, development agreements, minority equity investments, as well as joint ventures that are operated as separate legal entities. Joint ventures are normally created if parties involved want to form long-term relationships or an alliance will require significant investment in resources.

Why form strategic alliances?

- To penetrate new markets.
- To achieve faster penetration of markets.
- Reduce costs.
- Acquire new technology or knowledge-base.
- Gain design collaboration.
- Enhance competitiveness in global and domestic markets.
- Create new business.
- Achieve economies of scale.
- Sharing risks.
- Reduce cycle time.
- Improve quality.
- Complementing core competencies.

  Some examples of strategic alliance:

- In 2006 Microsoft Corp. and Nortel formed an alliance based on a shared vision for unified communications.

- Dell Computer Corporation formed an alliance with Sun Microsystems Inc.
- In 1997 Compaq Computer Corp formed an alliance with Intel Corp. to develop 100-megabit equipment. Compaq and Intel shared marketing and technical resources in order to achieve project objectives.
- In 1990, Hitachi and Hewlett-Packard (competitors) made an alliance to jointly develop and manufacture an advanced model of HP's Precision architecture RISC chip.
- Some airlines have come together to form an alliance to combine flight operations and dividing the markets.
- Food Science Australia formed an alliance with Singapore-based F & N Foods Pty Ltd to develop new products and processes.
- Alliance between Apple and IBM.
- Starbucks and books retailer Barnes and Noble.
- Fiat and Chrysler.

Alliances: Marketing perspective

'Place' is one of the key components of marketing mix. A firm has to consider very carefully what distribution method to use to reach its customers. Distributors in turn have to be careful in relation to the firm they are dealing with. They would want product delivered on time and in good condition and quality. Above all they are in business to make profit so they have considered what incentives they are being offered.

The trends these days to form network and alliances in order to reach consumers effectively. Various channels come together to form a network. These can be a vertical marketing integration where channel members function independently or relationship is based on contract. Horizontal channel integration occurs when one firm in a channel integrates with another channel at the same stage of distribution.

In order to enter markets swiftly **marketing alliances** are formed. Forming an alliance with another firm already established in a desired market region is faster and less costly than internal expansion or merger with another firm.

Global markets are becoming increasingly complex and competitive. Relatively few companies are now sufficiently large and have enough resources and skills to enter a completely new market through internal growth and using only their own resources.

According to Kotler and Keller (2006) (63), many strategic alliances take the form of marketing alliances. When one company licenses another company to produce its product or a service company markets its service with another service company it is known as product/service alliances.

When one firm promotes another firm's product or service, for example McDonalds promoting Disney films, then it is known as **promotional alliances**.

When one company offers logistical services for another company's product then it is known as **logistics alliances**. Finally, when firms collaborate on pricing offering mutual price discounts (airline firm and a hotel or car rental firm) then this is known as **pricing collaborations.**

Mergers need to be positioned properly to customers, employees and strategic partners. In addition, post-merger situation requires very thoughtful strategic marketing planning. Chief marketing officer has to play a key role in post-merger situations.

Mergers, acquisitions and alliances are important happenings for marketers. They involve dealing with customers in terms of achieving customer satisfaction, brand loyalty, customisation and personalisation, marketing strategy, value systems of organisations involved, relationship marketing, Public Relations, marketing communications and employment and redeployment of marketing resources.

Chapter Seven
Knowledge as a factor of production

In classical economics there are traditionally four factors of production. They are land, labour, capital and enterprise. Land involves all natural resources existing above and below the land. Labour consists of people engaged in producing goods and providing services. Capital includes machines and other physical assets needed to facilitate production of goods and provision of services. Enterprise co-ordinates all the named factors of production.

These factors are used to facilitate production. These four factors are still appropriate in modern world but now these factors have been extended to include knowledge and customers in order to reconnect economics with the realities of the modern business world. Also knowledge constitutes an important aspect of internal marketing.

Knowledge as such is an appreciating asset; the more it is used the more is created and the more effective its application. It incorporates the principle of increasing returns. The creation acquisition and effective deployment of knowledge in a firm has become the key source of competitive advantage. When we examine Gross Domestic products of countries like USA and UK, we find significant proportion of output is in the form of intangibles, based on the exploitation of ideas rather than material or tangible things. More and more goods from Mercedes cars to Nike trainers have increasing amounts of knowledge embedded in them, in the form of design, innovation and customer knowledge.

What is knowledge?

Knowledge in a nutshell is information *in use*. A distinction is made between data (a key aspect of digitised marketing), information and knowledge.

Data is unorganised word, numbers and images. It has no meaning and context as such. The name Sultan Kermally in a database is merely a data. Sultan Kermally is a regular customer of our products is information. Information is organised or categorised data. It has meaning or value added to data.

Knowledge is *use* of information. An organisation using information that Sultan Kermally is a regular customer of our products, take initiatives to establish special relationships with Sultan Kermally. It is using the information and thus creating customer knowledge —in this case knowledge about its customer Sultan Kermally. If the information gained is not used, then knowledge remains passive. It cannot be considered as an active intangible asset. Similarly, if employees have skills but he/she does not *use* them, then such skills remain passive and of no benefit to the organisation. Organisations, therefore, can gather/capture information about them. Customers about their employees about their competitors and thus become knowledge-driven organisation if they have the culture and processes to use the information. This is what knowledge management is all about.

Information and experiences of specific individuals are tacit knowledge. If the organisation puts processes in place to make this knowledge explicit so that other employees acquire this knowledge and use it then that organisation is facilitating knowledge creation and transfer. The initiatives that can be put in place include, coaching, shadowing, training workshops, after-action reviews, building skills directory and so on. The focus of attention in designing and introducing any initiative is to ask "does that initiative promote knowledge sharing - does it facilitate transformation of knowledge from being tacit or implicit to being explicit?"

Knowledge is the source of innovation. The application of knowledge enhances the capability of the organisation and the outcome brings about innovation. All forms of digitised information gathered these days' play key role instituting innovative processes and practice.

In practice there are many myths surrounding managing knowledge. They originate out of ignorance and prejudice. Some of the myths are as follows:

Myth No. 1

Knowledge management is about technology. Wrong. Knowledge as such has nothing to do with technology. Technology is merely an enabler. **Knowledge is about PEOPLE and how they are managed to collaborate and share their experiences and trust one another in exchanging knowledge gained.** Organisations require people at the top to secure and use knowledge. Technological developments and digitisation process enable individuals and organisations capture information but at the end of the day people decide how things should be done what should be done in practice.

Myth No. 2

Managing knowledge requires appointment of knowledge specialists and acquisition of knowledge systems. Wrong. Employees are 'knowledge workers' and what is needed is not the appointment of specialists but enthusiasts or knowledge champions. One does not require to purchase specialist's systems to manage knowledge. It is possible to manage knowledge without spending an additional dollar on computers or digital systems or so-called knowledge management systems.

Myth No. 3

Knowledge management is a fad and something very new advocated by consultants. Wrong. Knowledge management is not a fad; it is here to stay. It is also not new or it is as new as Egyptian pyramids. Some countries and organisations have been managing knowledge for a number of years. For example 3M and Skandia have been managing knowledge for a number of years. 3M, since they have started doing business, have managed to sustain innovation by encouraging employees to share their knowledge and Skandia, as a result of their experience in managing knowledge, have highlighted the importance of human capital in assessing the performance of their organisation. It has become imperative now for all organisations including SMEs because of globalisation and internationalisation of businesses and markets. **We now do business in market space as opposed to market place**. Various publications from academics and consultants focus on the way organisations should approach a process of knowledge creation and sharing.

Why managing knowledge has become important for all organisations now?

Organisations now face the following challenges:

- Increasing value of the intellectual capital is embedded in end products and services.
- There has been and is increasing convergence of technologies and digitisation that is enabling organisations to globalise at the press of the button.
- There is a rapid growth of Internet.

In summary *"Economies are increasingly based on knowledge.... What is new is that a growing chunk of production in the modern economy is in the form of intangibles, based on the exploitation of ideas rather than material things..."* (64)

Many organisations are resisting adopting knowledge management initiative and system because most of them have gone through the traumas of re engineering, de-layering and restructuring, mergers and acquisitions. Some of the employees have gone through difficult times over the past three decades. They do not want or are not ready to jump through yet another hoop.

However, the way business is structured nowadays and with the advent of the Digital Economy managing knowledge has become business imperative if the organisations have to gain and sustain competitive advantage. Knowledge in our current atmosphere (in relation to Big data, the Internet of Everything, the Cloud computing) has become the source and the result of data analysis.

Given that, it is imperative what is meant by managing knowledge?

Managing knowledge

There are as many definitions of knowledge management as there are experts in this area. In basic terms managing knowledge is about creating an environment where people within the organisation trust one another and trust leadership to share and create knowledge so that organisations can win new businesses and compete efficiently. Organisations in this respect will be investing in internal marketing. Creating such an environment involves changing the culture of the organisation and putting processes in place to enable knowledge creation and transfer.

Making a start. Some examples/initiatives

Begin to build an experience directory. If, for example, you are a project management company then do ask each of your employees to some key questions, say about ten questions after they have experienced completion of the project. The questions should draw out the nature of the project, the challenges involved and the way these challenges were attended to and the person/persons involved in the project. The result will be the creation of the experience directory. The information should be made available to all project leaders. Such an initiative will stop reinventing a wheel, save cost and encourage exchange of information and creation of organisational knowledge.

The other initiative would be to capture information on what employees currently do, what they could do given the opportunity and what they would like to do (their aspirations) given the opportunity to acquire new skills.

The organisation can transform this information in formulating stretch objectives for their employees and for preparing developmental objectives that could be used for new business development.

Knowledge is also power. Why should employees share this power?

Knowledge is an appreciating asset. The more it is shared the more it is enhanced. If an organisation has an effective leadership and if the culture of organisation is conducive to people trusting one another then employees or 'knowledge-workers' will be glad to 'empower' them colleagues by sharing their knowledge. At the end of the day whether the organisation becomes the Knowledge-driven organisation depends on leadership, culture and *trust*.

There are many examples in practice of some organisations and teams creating initiatives to share and create knowledge without individual or organisational tears. Many publications give examples of organisations include Sun Microsystems, Microsoft, Chevron, Xerox, Bankers Trust, and Shell. Employees have come together to create knowledge for them organisations.

Here are the examples of mini past cases over the past few years to illustrate the importance of managing knowledge.

British petroleum

Sir John Browne former CEO of British Petroleum established a team to facilitate learning both within and across the flattened hierarchy. He emphasised the importance of 'dual citizenship' meaning that every employee should be loyal and think about the good of his or her group as well as to the group as a whole. Employees were encouraged to record their experience capturing key events before, during and after each project and record lessons learnt on corporate intranet.

Such a practice enabled capturing of significant information which employees could use to deliver desired results and it had impact on reducing costs as the practice of re-inventing the wheel was reduced.

It is reported that by creating and managing knowledge, BP speeded up refinery turnaround, discovered new oil and gas field, accelerated new market entry and improved plant reliability. The approach resulted in around 4260 million of added value.

Chevron Corp

Chevron Corp based in San Francisco long way back in 1980s established groupware technology to facilitate knowledge sharing and transfer, first within the business sector and then trough out the group. Employees were encouraged to share best practices. Using such best practices resulted into high performance in the development of world and production-related innovations such as horizontal drilling and three-dimensional, seismic exploration in order to meet its objectives.

Shell

Shell adopted various methods and techniques to manage knowledge. It is reported that they made millions of dollars in saving including repairs worth $1.5 million on well casings and electrical submersible pumps by Petroleum Development Oman through knowledge sharing from Shell Oil.

Xerox Corporation

Knowledge managers were appointed to lead initiatives in the USA and Europe. Their responsibilities included capturing information on where technology was going, where consumers were going and what geographies were changing.

Xerox service technicians come across various challenges in making service calls. The company developed a special system to capture these challenges and experiences. This resulted into savings of 5 to 10% in labour and parts costs.

There are numerous success stories of organisations which have benefited from managing knowledge effectively.

Knowledge is intangible asset which an organisation can use to achieve cost savings and gain competitive advantage. The modern firm has to have such objectives in their strategy in order to survive and thrive in a global arena. It is not just the question of land, labour capital and enterprise any more but factor such as labour has to be analysed to examine its nature within the context of modern business. Wages and productivity which were emphasised in economics are important but one also has to look at labour as one of the components of marketing mix and as source of knowledge creation within the firm.

Process of knowledge creation

Since knowledge is one of the key significant assets the firm has to compete effectively, it is important to understand the process of knowledge creation within the firm.

There are two types of knowledge, namely **tacit knowledge** and **explicit knowledge.** Tacit knowledge is a personal knowledge that is the knowledge that is in our head. This is key aspect of the labour as a factor of production. The other type is explicit knowledge which has been articulated and recorded or coded. When, for example a service technician uses his or her experience to resolve a problem then he/she is using tacit knowledge. After resolving the problem, he/she records it for others to use he/she has been it explicit. The recorded information becomes explicit knowledge when used.

Nonaka and Takeuchi (1995) (65) gurus of managing knowledge presented a model of knowledge creation and transfer within an organisation. The model has four interacting stages. They are **socialisation stage, externalisation stage, combination stage** and **internalisation stage**.

Socialisation stage starts with individuals. At this stage an organisation has to have processes in place to capture tacit knowledge of individuals and transform this tacit knowledge into group or team tacit knowledge.

The transfer is facilitated by sharing experiences and on-the-job training and learning. They give an example of Matsushita's development of an automatic bread machine. In the late 1980s its software engineers apprenticed themselves to the head baker of the Osaka International Hotel. The baker was reputed to produce the area's best bread. The engineers discovered that the baker was not only stretching but also twisting the dough in a particular fashion which turned out to be the secret for making tasty bread. Subsequently the practice was incorporated into the machine for making bread.

The firm at this stage had to put various initiatives in its place in order to encourage face-to-face sharing of work-related project experience. Such initiative would include seminars and workshops, customer interaction, coaching and mentoring.

Externalisation stage involves converting a tacit knowledge into explicit knowledge. At this stage models and prototypes are created to embed tacit knowledge into products. For example, some food companies invite customers to taste food (food tasting panels) to see that they have got it right before manufacturing for mass market.

Recently a TV documentary showed how the tacit knowledge of heart surgeons has embedded in robots by way of programming robots to perform heart surgery as long as a heart surgeon was in control of robots.

Combination stage involves embedding the combination of knowledge gained in the socialisation and externalisation stages into final product. 'How to' manuals and instructions are prepared as a result of this stage.

In the case of food producing companies once they do food tasting then finally decide on recipes and produce recipes books.

Internalisation stage involves transforming explicit knowledge into tacit knowledge. A cook for example, follows a recipe in a recipe book and over time he or she is able to produce food without referring to the recipe book. He/she has internalised the recipe requirements. This stage is about 'learning by doing.'

To be knowledge-driven organisation, appropriate processes have to be put in place so that individuals have opportunity to share and use knowledge.

Nonaka (1991) presented the Japanese perspective on the use of knowledge as a factor of production. He wrote:

"In an economy where the only certainty is uncertainty, the only sure source of lasting competitive advantage is knowledge. When markets shift, technologies proliferate, competitors multiply, and products become obsolete almost overnight, successful companies are those that consistently create knowledge, disseminate it widely throughout the organisation, and quickly embody it in new technologies and products. These activities define the 'knowledge-creating' company, whose sole business is continuous innovation." (66)

Building Marketing Knowledge. Improving effectiveness of internal marketing

What kind of information should marketer focus on and how can they create and manage knowledge, an economic asset?

Marketing is well placed to manage knowledge effectively as in marketing there are various frameworks and models which marketer use to gather information. These models include S.W.O.T. Analysis, S.T.E.E.P. Analysis, Ansoff's matrix, Product Portfolio matrix, General Electric Strategic Planning Matrix, Shell Directional Policy Matrix and others. In fact, marketers are very good in gathering and processing information. It is important, however, for them to manage knowledge and use it as a factor of production to bring about innovation in products, to penetrate new markets, to accelerate speedy entrance to markets and to achieve 'strategic fit' for their organisations.

The following sections will deal with three frameworks, namely S.W.O.T framework, Environmental Analysis Framework and Impact Analysis framework to gather information and to transform such information into knowledge.

S.W.O.T. Analysis

S.W.O.T. stands for strengths, weaknesses, opportunities and threats. The firm, in order to assess its capabilities to compete effectively and respond to changes taking place can undertake S.W.O.T. analysis.

Strengths and weaknesses focus on internal resources of the firm. They relate to systems, processes, staff, skills, culture, leadership, communication and so on. The objective is to focus on getting information on these internal aspects of the firm in order to assess its capabilities to deliver strategic objectives.

Opportunities relate to external environment. The assessment has to be made on what changes are taking place in the environment, environmental as well as competitive, within which business is done and then assessment is made to see whether internal capabilities exist to take advantage of opportunities and respond to threats. The information on opportunities and threats can be obtained from conducting environmental analysis known as S.T.E.E.P. (Sociological, Technological, Economic, Environmental and Political) analysis.

The information gathered is of no use to the firm unless it is used to take appropriate actions. The firm might have to fine tune or reformulate its strategies or acquire resources and new skills or both in order to achieve 'strategic fit.' The knowledge created by using information will enable firm to achieve its strategic objectives.

Conducting S.T.E.E.P. Analysis

Surveying social, technological, economic, environmental and political factors provide information on the opportunities available to the firm and the threats facing the firm.

Social factors relate to changes taking place in a society. Changes in population, its composition, its mobility, the attitude of people, social values, changes in life styles the role of women and other minorities and so on all have impact on business —favourably or unfavourably. For example, ageing population will prompt insurance companies in coming up with products that would be attractive to older people. It will provide marketers in designing appropriate segments to market new products.

Ageing population present the global challenge. In 1990 almost 500 million people (more than 9 per cent of the world population) were more than 60 years old. The World Bank estimated that by 2030 the number will be 1.4 billion. Such changes will provide opportunities to some firms and threats to others if they are unwilling or unable to adapt to these changes.

Changing attitude towards using mobile phones has accelerated the demand for mobile phones. Nowadays it does not matter where you go in the country or to other countries one cannot get away from mobile phones.

Technological factors

Technology is developing at dramatic rate. Product life cycles of certain goods such as software products are being squeezed dramatically due to the accelerating pace of technological developments. Such development impacts all aspects of our life.

Advances in general purpose computing are allowing users to create and use extremely sophisticated applications. Such applications create new capabilities and opportunities.

Everyone is familiar with internet and yet less than two decades ago it was unthinkable that an international network could grow so dramatically at breath taking pace. Few years ago Fortune magazine ran a story to show how the internet has penetrated Europe's most remote spots – geographically (Lapland) as well as demographically (the homeless) – libraries in Budapest for example, provide free access.

The internet facilitates the speed of information and creates markets where buyers and suppliers come together. It enables companies to reinvent themselves and it slashes time and costs out of the supply chain. Above all it provides global reach in marketing.

Businesses respond to these technological developments in order to compete effectively in a global climate. 'Bricks' organisations like Ford, General Motors, general Electric are transformation to become what is known as 'clicks' organisation.

New technologies and their falling costs have become the important catalysts in changing the way business is being conducted. In relation to market, managing digital technologies involves managing the implementation and ongoing operations of these technologies.

Nowadays we live in a world of 'cyberspace.' We can create information and do analysis in a speed of time. Organisations deal with Big Data which is characterised by **volume** (the amount of information in existence and in creation, **variety** (the diversity of information provided) and **velocity** (the speed of knowledge creation and analytical actions taken. Conventional approach to gathering data and analysing data has been transformed by the use of digital media and various data analytical tools to analyse aspects of Big data in order to create useful information within the context of managing knowledge.

Economic factors

The factors include macro-economic variables such as employment, inflation, exchange rates, interest rates, economic growth and so on. The economic landscape is also changing dramatically.

Few years ago the biggest crisis facing the economy in the USA and UK was the crisis facing mortgage lenders including banks and building societies which have involved in sub-prime mortgages. Houses are being re-possessed due to inability of householders to meet their mortgage commitments. The experts in the UK were predicting recession and we did suffer and in some instance still suffering the bad effects of the crisis.

Many businesses are already responding by making their employees redundant which in time will have knock-on effect on demand for goods and services. Sometimes the best-crafted strategies of businesses are frustrated by economic factors where the sources of instability come from outside the country. The sub-prime mortgage crisis started in the USA and in a very short time its impact is felt in the UK. In a global environment when one country sneezes the other countries catch pneumonia.

Hopefully in some countries like UK and USA the economic situation is improving and this situation should provide incentive to investing in knowledge creation system.

Environmental factors

These factors known as 'Green issues' are making impact on businesses and customers are becoming more demanding in terms of environmental issues.

Many societies are now concerned about the environmental and ecological factors such as emission and safety standards, recycling and pollution levels. Manufacturers are 'forced' to adapt their processes and embrace new technologies in response to customer demands.

If we take example of food, shelf life is consumers' convenience and yet the pressure on manufacturers is to get rid of artificial additives (used to prolong shelf life) which can induce hyperactivity in young children.

Recycling has also become a big issue. Coca Cola now owns various recycling plants across the world. The company is stepping up efforts to recycle plastic containers amid growing backlash against the sale of bottled water in the US and the UK.

Political factors

These factors influence business strategy and the way businesses are conducted nationally and internationally. Political climate is changing from conflict to co-operation. Geographic barriers are ceasing to be barriers to doing trade. Governments in many countries are privatising and de-regulating public sector businesses.

Since the fall Berlin wall and the abandonment of Communism, there have been steady streams of mergers, acquisitions and alliances across borders. Many attempts are being made at different Governmental conferences to liberalise trade not only in relation to manufactured goods but also services.

Scanning environment within which businesses operate will generate information which can then be processed to create knowledge by using information to come up with new products, new processes, innovative marketing in order to capture opportunities available and to take appropriate actions such as deploying various strategic options such as mergers, alliances and forming strategic partnerships to fend off threats. Information in use is what management knowledge is all about. In using know new experience is gained and existing knowledge is enhanced. Hence knowledge is viewed as appreciating asset. The more knowledge is used and shared the more knowledge is created. Knowledge combined with technology can transform the whole business.

Once again it is important to emphasise that knowledge management is people-based. It is important for all sizes of business in public as well private sectors. In a paper written by The Economist Intelligence Unit and sponsored by Tata Consultancy Services (2005) they give various examples of organisations such as Schlumberger, Tesco, Wanadoo, BBC and Barclays who have benefited from going into managing knowledge. The Economist Intelligence Unit conducted a survey of 122 senior executives in Western Europe 68 of whom were based in the UK. In conclusion they stated:

"Like most intangibles, knowledge is a tricky thing to manage. But there are plenty of examples that prove that, with a sound approach to knowledge management, companies can translate their information assets into real value for the business...." (67)

Marketing knowledge

In relation to Marketing and Economics, few publications have come out focussing on using marketing knowledge. According to Kohlbacher (2007),

"Marketing knowledge is all knowledge, both declarative as well as procedural, concerning marketing thinking and behaviour in a corporation." In this publication the author also gives the definition of marketing knowledge given by Pollard (2006) (68) *"marketing knowledge of a company develops both in-house and through external contact." Kohlbacher states that "both definitions include both tacit and explicit knowledge about products, markets, customers, partners, marketing processes and marketing strategy."* (69)

By managing knowledge effectively marketers can focus on numerous aspects of organisational operations and effectiveness including segmenting markets effectively, Branding products and services, Relationship marketing, Developing new products and competitive advantage. In this age of digitisation all knowledge is digitisable can be used effectively by the help of various digital media, channels and platforms.

Chapter Eight
Globalisation

In economic terms, globalisation means economic interdependence between trading countries. Over the years various institutions such as the European Union, North American Free Trade Agreement, World Trade Organisation, World Bank, International Monetary Fund and other institutions have been established to promote world trade and economic integration and co-operation. Globalisation cannot be understood properly without examining some of the institutions developed in order to promote trade between countries and to remove barriers to trade. In this context references will be made very briefly to the development of International Monetary Fund (IMF), World Trade Organisation, (WTO), North American Free trade agreement (NAFTA) and the European Union (EU).

International Monetary Fund

In 1944, delegates from forty-four countries met in Bretton Woods, New Hampshire, USA to establish a system of fixed exchange rates in order to promote the growth of world trade. The organisation established to manage this system was called the International Monetary Fund. US dollar was the key currency as most international trade and finance were carried out in dollars and payments were made out in dollars. Exchange-rate parities were set in dollar terms. International trade grew rapidly and many countries' economies prospered. They began to build dollar balances which subsequently put strain on dollars and the US in 1971 made a decision to sever the link between dollars and other currencies. Since then some countries adopted flexible exchange rates while some countries in Europe joined together to stabilise their exchange rates among themselves. Thus was created the European Monetary System.

Being tied to the European Monetary System meant that countries belonging to it had to give up control over their monetary policies. During the period 1989 and 1993 some countries belonging to the system began to experience economic crisis which led to the demise of European Monetary System.

To date IMF, known also as the Fund, has 189 countries as members. The Fund main aims are (a) to facilitate international trade (b) promote high employment (c) promote exchange stability (d) encourage sustainable economic growth and (e) reduce poverty.

In 2015 IMF faced challenges in relation to decline in oil prices affecting oil producing countries, Ebola pandemic in Guinea, Liberia and Sierra Leone and helping several member countries addressing difficult economic and financial circumstances. For more information, read IMF Report 2015 (70).

World Trade Organisation

The World Trade Organisation was created in 1995. Its main objectives are to liberalise trade and where necessary support barriers to trade in order to protect consumers, spread diseases and protect environment.

Before the establishment of WTO, the General Agreement on Tariffs and Trade (GATT) provided the rules for much of the world trade during the period 1948 to 1994. The first agreements in relation to trade rules and tariff concessions   concluded under GATT took place in 1947 in Geneva.

According to the World Trade Organisation website, (71) there was also an intention to create International Trade Organisation (ITO) to handle the trade side of the international economic cooperation. The draft charter included rules on employment, commodity agreements, restrictive practices, international investment and services. The charter was agreed in 1948 but in 1950 the US did not agree to ratify it. GATT became the main instrument of trade regulation till the creation of World Trade Organisation. It played a key part in liberalising much of the world trade. However, due to the growth of the service sector (services were not covered by GATT rules) and the process of globalisation it was decided to create a new institution to deal with a new emerging international economic situation. Thus was created World Trade Organisation (WTO).

At its heart are the WTO agreements, negotiated and signed by the bulk of the world's trading nations and ratified in their parliaments. The goal is to help producers of goods and services, exporters, and importers conduct their business.

Under the WTO agreements, countries cannot normally discriminate between their trading partners. If one country grants a concession to another country, then it must also offer concessions equally to all other member countries. This is known as Most-favoured-nation (MFN) clause. It was also the first principle under GATT Agreements. In practice some exceptions are allowed for example, making concessions to some developing countries.

The second principle relates to treating foreigners and locals equally. Imported and locally-produced goods and services should be treated equally.

Under WTO rules when countries agree to open their markets for goods and services, they 'bind' their commitments. The multilateral trading system I an attempt by governments to make economic environment stable, predictable and transparent.

In January, 2016, WTO released new statistical profiles on global value chains.

"Using data from the OECD-WTO database on Trade in Value Added (ITiva), these profiles provide insights into the value-added content of exports, the interconnection between economies within GVCs and the role of the services industry in exports. Other indicators related to GVCs include trade in intermediate goods, trade facilitation and foreign direct investment."(72)

North American Free Trade Agreement (NAFTA)(73)

The North American Free Trade Agreement (NAFTA) was created by the governments of the United States, Canada and Mexico in 1994. The objective of the agreement was to remove most barriers to trade and investment among the three countries party to the agreement.

Under the agreement, all non-tariff barriers to agricultural trade between the United States and Mexico were eliminated. The same applied to tariffs affecting agricultural trade between the United States and Canada. Mexico and Canada reached a separate bilateral NAFTA agreement on market access for agricultural products.

The final provisions of NAFTA were fully implemented on January 1, 2008. This meant elimination of the remaining trade restrictions between the United States and Mexico.

The European Union

The European Union was formerly known as the European Economic Community (EEC) and it was established under the Treaty of Rome in 1957 and entered into force on January 1, 1958. The original members of the Union were France, West Germany, Italy, Belgium, the Netherlands and Luxembourg. In 1973, the United Kingdom, Ireland and Denmark joined in followed by Greece, Spain and Portugal in the 1980s.In 1990 after the fall of the Iron Curtain, the former East Germany became part of the Community as part of a newly united Germany.

In 1993, the European Union was formally established when the Maastricht Treaty came into force in November, 1993 and in 1995 Austria, Sweden and Finland joined the European Union.

The main objectives of the Union are to create Single Market that would facilitate free movement of goods, services, capital and people and the application of common external tariff on all goods entering the market. Once the goods have entered into the market they cannot be subjected to custom duties, discriminatory taxes or import quotas.

In 2002 euro note and coins replaced national currencies in 12 member states. The Eurozone at present consist of 19 countries. All other members of the Union except the United Kingdom and Denmark are legally bound to join the euro when the economic conditions are met.

The European Union at present (October, 2015) consist of 28 member states. The members are Austria, Belgium, Bulgaria, Croatia, Cyprus Chez Republic, Denmark, Estonia, Finland, France, Germany, Greece, Hungary, Ireland, Italy, Latvia, Lithuania, Luxembourg Malta, the Netherlands, Poland, Portugal, Romania, Slovakia, Spain, Sweden, United Kingdom. As far as United Kingdom is concerned there will be a national referendum on 23rd. June, 2016 where British people will be given a referendum to vote whether to remain in the European or not. This will be the most important socio-economic decision made in relation to the membership of the European Union.

European revenue comes from (a) contribution in relation to a small percentage of Gross National Income from member countries (b) EU country's standardised value added tax, (c) a large share of import duties on non-EU products.

According to the information provided by the European Union, it is the world's biggest trader accounting for 16.5% of world's imports and exports. The Euro is the official currency and it is used by 19 out of 28 member countries. These countries are collectively known as Eurozone.

Enter globalisation

Late Peter Drucker once told the marketing audience *'While you were out, the world changed.'*

Since 1980, the rapid growth of both international trade and capital flows has enabled many large businesses and financial institutions to go global in their outlook and organisation. The contributory forces of globalisation are technological advances such as the convergence of computing and telecommunications, deregulation of business and financial markets, privatisation associated with abandonment of communist ideological outlook and the escalation of cross-border capital flows such as bank lending, international bond issues and mutual fund portfolio investments.

These trends are integrating the world economy in the flow of goods, services, capital and people.

The economic aspects of globalisation are related to trade, finance and migration. From trade perspective, one can go to any supermarket and by mangoes from India, guavas from Africa, pineapple from Malaysia, and coffee from Colombia and so on. Consumers now have access to goods and services all over the world. Globalisation has become a process; it is seen as more than just doing trade or running financial markets.

According to Yip (2012), (74) there are four categories of drivers that determine the extent of globalisation within an industry. These categories are **market drivers, cost drivers, government drivers** and **competitive drivers**.

Market drivers are determined by customer needs which in turn are influenced by cultural and economic convergence. Big manufacturers source materials globally and as a consequence create global distributors' network.

Producers are creating brands and consolidate them globally. Certain countries like Japan and USA which take the lead in innovation establish global standards. Marketing communications in relation to global products and service are designed to meet local variations but maintaining global status.

Cost drivers relate economies of scale and economies of scope. Global markets are large and producing for large markets facilitate various economies of scale which impact upon cost of production.

Economies of scope are gained because often products share the same distribution outlets or some of them are packaged together, for example air travel and hotel accommodation. Global economies of scale drive industry towards globalisation.

Global sourcing, logistics, global talent, high productivity all contribute to accelerate globalisation process.

Sources of government drivers are government policies in relation to liberalising trade, deregulating industry, and privatisation, establishing common technical standards, advertising, subsidies and protection.

Competitive drivers relate to interdependence between countries. The level of exports and imports will indicate the extent of globalisation. Businesses facing competitors globally will be forced to compete globally thus accentuating globalisation process.

From comparative advantage to competitive advantage

In economics the concept of comparative advantage is at the heart of international trade. According to the theory of comparative cost advantage, countries can benefit from trade even if it is absolutely more efficient (or absolutely less efficient) than other countries in the production of every good.

If country 'A' is more efficient in producing goods 'X' and 'Y' compared to country 'B,' according to the theory of the comparative cost advantage, as long as country 'A' is relatively more efficient in producing good 'X' than 'Good 'Y,' it will benefit country 'A' in concentrating in producing good 'X' and exporting it to other countries and importing good 'Y.' According to the principle of comparative advantage, each country trading will gain if it specialises in the production of goods which they can produce at relatively low cost and export them. The countries should import those goods which can be produced at high cost.

In relation to the theory of comparative advantage, it is the opportunity cost that matters. Decision to trade is based on the basis of opportunity cost. Country 'A' will benefit from trade if it is able to obtain good from other country by giving up less than it would have to give up to obtain the good at home.

The theory dates back to classical economist David Ricardo. It is one of the most widely accepted among economists.

The theory of comparative advantage is based on the productivity and cost differences of the traditional factors of production, namely land, labour, capital and enterprise and it also depends on resource endowments. In the modern economy we also have to consider other factors such as knowledge, core competencies and customers. Instead of comparative advantage we need to focus on competitive advantage.

According to Porter (1985) (75), competitive advantage is at the heart of a firm's performance in competitive markets. How organisations at micro level generic strategies involving cost leadership, differentiation and focus to position themselves in a competitive arena is what the modern business is all about and it is also how businesses trade internationally.

Porter (1985) wrote:

"Competitive advantage cannot be understood by looking at a firm as a whole. It stems from the many discrete activities a firm performs in designing, producing, marketing delivering, and supporting its product. Each of these activities can contribute to a firm's relative cost position and create a basis for differentiation." (76)

Value chain analysis is applicable to goods as well as services. According to Grant (1991) (77), one can also apply value chain analysis from customer perspective. The customer's value chain begins with search activity before purchase is made. Value chain activities for manufacturers and consumers in practice are complex.

Marketing perspective

Marketers can use value chain analysis to:

- Analyse organisational capabilities to undertake effective marketing;
- Use to analyse costs;
- Eliminate non-value adding activities thus reduce costs;
- Benchmark against competitors' value chains;
- Configure value chains to take advantage of e-commerce;
- Make outsourcing decisions;
- Assess opportunities to form strategic alliances.

Marketers have to conduct competitive analysis before formulating business and marketing strategies to compete globally. Marketers can use **Porter's Five Forces Analysis** to understand competitive climate and to formulate appropriate strategies. This analysis is important as it has to be conducted within the context of globalisation.

Porter's Five Force Analysis. In 1979 Michael Porter put forward his Five Force Analysis model to explain the nature of strategic competitiveness. According to Porter, in any industry the rules of the competition are governed by five competitive forces. They are:

1. Potential entrants.
2. Competitive rivalry.
3. Substitutes.
4. The bargaining power of buyers.
5. The bargaining power of suppliers.

These five forces address the question 'why are some markets more attractive than others?' The collective strength of these five competitive forces determines the ability of firms in an industry to earn, on average, return on investment in excess of the cost of capital.

What constitute these forces? The following is the summary of Porter's Five Forces tool.

Potential entrants

Potential entrant to any market has to overcome various barriers. These include economies of scale and economies of scope, product and service differentiation, access to distribution channels, dedicated plant, and access to raw materials, brand identity, switching costs, proprietary products, complex technology and government policy.

Competitive rivalry

Competitive rivalry depends on industry concentration, brand identity, switching costs, product differences, industry growth, margins, market share, credibility to integrate forward and backwards, exit barriers, profitability and number and diversity of firms competing.

Threat of substitutes

These substitutes from other industries. These relate to products available, which products offer better price, and performance of products.

The bargaining power of buyers

This relate to the demands for quality, bargaining leverage, buyer volume, price insensitivity, threat of backward integration, product differentiation, availability of substitutes.

In economics when the buying power is strong, the relationship to the producing industry is termed as monopsony. This is a situation where there are too many buyers but only one buyer.

The bargaining power of suppliers

This relates to profitability of supplying firms, can suppliers integrate forward? Capacity and utilisation, supplier concentration, differentiation of inputs and cost relative to total purchases in industry.

These are five key forces influencing intensity of competitiveness in any industry. The important thing to remember is that these forces are not static. Business environment is dynamic and this is why firms should assume continuous improvement mindset. Conducting macro-economic environment analysis (S.T.E.E.P. Analysis), SWOT Analysis and Five Forces Analysis will enable a firm to review its strategies constantly to gain '**strategic fit.**' Marketers have to be innovative in their approach and thinking to gain and sustain competitive advantage.

Having conducted various analyses, businesses then have to focus on appropriate strategies to focus on competitive advantage.

In order to focus on competitive advantage rather than comparative advantage, Porter has proposed the following strategies which are termed as **generic strategies**. The understanding of these generic strategies is very important to marketer. Without such an understanding marketing strategies could be ineffective and expensive. The following generic strategies were published in 1985 in his book *'Competitive Advantage: Creating and Sustaining Superior Performance.'*

Cost leadership

In this situation an organisation sets out to be the low-cost producer in its industry. It caters for many industry segments. If an organisation can achieve and sustain overall cost leadership, then it will achieve superior performance. Cost leadership can be obtained by focusing on key accounts, achieving economies of scale and economies of scope, out sourcing and global sourcing and organisational restructuring.

Differentiation

This strategic focus would involve an organisation in providing something unique to its target customers. The uniqueness can be related to products, the way it is delivered, the way it is augmented and enhanced, the way it markets and the way it communicates to shape customers' perception of the products or services. This could be the way products and services are branded or designed and customers perceive such offerings as unique.

According to Grant (1991) (78) differentiation is not the same as segmentation. Differentiation is concerned with how each organisation competes. The firm has to offer its uniqueness to customers. Such uniqueness might relate to consistency, reliability, quality and innovation. The firm has to decide on differentiation and incorporate its decision in strategic planning.

Focus strategy

This strategy involves an organisation in being selective in terms of the segments it wants to serve and focusing on these segments to the exclusion of other segments. The focus strategy can either be cost focus or differentiation focus. It can concentrate on a narrow segment and within that segment achieve either cost advantage or differentiation.

Generic strategies affect the following aspects of marketing:

- Costs and pricing.
- Product design.
- Marketing mix.
- Channels of distribution.
- Promotion.
- Segmentation.
- Branding.
- Marketing information.
- Marketing communication.

Globalisation has facilitated and continues to facilitate access to global markets for goods and services. It has also opened worldwide financial markets and financial instruments to finance trade across the world.

It has also been triggered off by the establishment of economic and financial institutions which in turn is being consolidated and adopted in response to globalisation process.

There is much more freedom of goods and services now than has been the case three decades ago. Ecologically also there has been a favourable impact as a result of global co-operation.

Globalisation has enabled the understanding of multi-culturalism and marketers now a day has to pay special attention to diversity and multi-cultural issues in designing their products and services and in communicating to customers globally. This aspect of marketing is dealt with in the chapters on advertising and marketing communications.

The advantages of globalisation

Globalisation brings a number of potential benefits to international producers and national economies.

Expanding the scope of the markets, organisations could gain the following benefits:

1. Access to raw materials at a low cost
2. Increase specialisation in division of labour
3. Specialisation increases the national income of each country
4. Capturing higher profit opportunities
5. Enhance customer base
6. Counterattack global competitors
7. Overcoming trade regulations

Disadvantages of globalisation include:

1. Taking high risks
2. Over-standardisation of products

3. Potential loss of jobs in domestic markets
4. Misunderstanding of foreign country's culture
5. Shortage of international managerial skills
6. Political uncertainty
7. Occurrence of contagion effects in relation to economic crisis

Critics of globalisation point out that all the benefits of globalisation have accrued to wealthy and developed nations. Increasingly poor nations are suffering and there is a move now to use the benefits created by globalisation to help such nations. Countries like India and China are growing at dramatic rates as a result of globalisation and it is argued their growth is contributing to increase in pollution. Globalisation creates winners and losers.

It is important to note that **globalisation is a process and not the destiny.** In the past two decades the breadth and depth of links between various countries have taken place and digitisation is accelerating global links internationally. In Davos in November, 2015 various economists, politicians, and all types of campaigners will meet to discuss formally and informally issues related to sustainable development, income inequality and climate change. Various economic issues relating to globalisation come alive during this stage. Marketers have to pay special attention to the issues and developments in order to gather information and creating marketing knowledge.

Current situation after Financial Crisis of 2007-2008

Financial crisis of 2007-2008 also known as global financial crisis has been described as the worst financial crisis since the Great Depression of the 1930s. According to Wikipedia (79) it threatened the collapse of large financial institutions, which was prevented by the bailout of banks by national governments, but stock markets still dropped worldwide. In many areas, the housing market also suffered, resulting in evictions, foreclosures and prolonged unemployment. The crisis played a significant role in the failure of key businesses, declines in consumer wealth estimated in trillions of U.S. dollars, and a downturn in economic activity leading to the 2008-2012 global recession and contributing to the European sovereign-debt crisis. The active phase of the crisis, which manifested as a liquidity crisis, can be dated from August 9, 2007, when BNP Paribas terminated withdrawals from three hedge funds citing "a complete evaporation of liquidity. The crisis was caused by numerous factors including the following:

- The breakdown of the housing bubble in the USA
- Easier access to loans
- Provision of complex financial products
- Failure in financial regulation
- Weak mortgage lending standards
- Low interest rates
- Weak regulatory pressure

Financial institutions suffered enormously and various governments had to initiate bail out programmes for them.

World trade has fallen by the largest amount since the financial crisis of 2007-2008. In June, 2015 Financial Times reported:

> *"We have had a miserable first six months of 2015," said Robert Koopmans, chief economist of the World Trade Organisation, which has forecast 3.3 per cent growth in the volume of global trade this year but is likely to revise that estimate down in coming weeks."* (80)

Prior to financial crisis in 2007-2008, experts were predicting the growth of economic power in countries like Brazil, Russia, India and China. This was referred to as **BRIC economies**. Goldman Sachs economist Jim O' Neill used the acronym BRIC representing Brazil, Russia, India and China to predict the development of big emerging markets taking place in these four countries. This was predicted in 2001. These countries would be economically wealthier than most of the current economic powers. In 2010 South Africa joined BRIC to become BRICS economies.

According to Global Sherpa. Org, *"From 2000 to 2008, the BRIC countries' combined share of total world economic output rose from 16 to 22 percent. Together, the BRIC countries accounted for 30 percent of the increase in global output during the period."* (81)

> *To date, the scale of China's economy and pace of its development has out-distanced those of its BRIC peers. China alone contributed more than half of the BRIC countries' share and greater than 15 percent of the growth in world economic output from 2000 to 2008."*

The key statistics of various economic factors and development are given in Wikipedia. The BRICS countries still hold their annual summits. The 7th Summit was held in Russia in July 2015. BRICS have also opened their New Development Bank (NDB) with its headquarters based in Shanghai. The NDB rivals the World Bank and IMF.

Some experts are now also putting forward countries like Mexico, Turkey, Indonesia and South Korea to join BRICS. The other acronym created now is MINT representing Mexico, India, Nigeria and Turkey.

How is BRICS doing now? According to Rana Foroohar's article:

> *"Why the Mighty BRIC Nations Have Finally Broken? (2015) there have been numerous factors contributed to such downs in some of these countries. However, China is seen to be making bigger contribution to the world economic market and will be predicted to remain so for some time to come. Foroohar concludes."* (82)

Brazil's economic growth has slowed down over the last four years. Inflation has been running in double digits. It is important for Brazil to focus more on achieving better economic growth and improve its competitiveness.

Russia is experiencing recession. The country is suffering due to the fall in oil and gas prices and also the sanctions imposed by the West are impacting unfavourably on economic progression.

India currently is doing well in economic terms. The economy is on the stable footing. The economic growth rate is at the moment faster than that in China. World Bank and IMF are forecasting India to grow faster than China.

China is currently experiencing lower economic growth. Unemployment is rising as a result of employees in construction and mining losing their jobs. The economic plan at the moment is focussing on improving its economic growth rate.

South Africa is experiencing lower economic growth. The unemployment currently is 25% and the country is experiencing high inflation rate.

Indeed, what happens in the BRICS and the rest of the emerging markets over the next few months will have as much to do with the Fed as with China—as America's central bank raised rates, which will inevitably strengthen the dollar, many emerging market nations and companies with dollar pegged economies and dollar denominated debt will come under pressure. That may break more than just the BRICs.

Globalisation is a process and not the destination. BRICS, MINT and other countries in developing and developed world would play key role in globalisation process.

Chapter Nine
Economics of Advertising and Promotion

Advertising is dealt separately in economics but in marketing it is part of promotional mix and promotion is one of the key components of marketing mix.

Advertising

In practice most firms operate in a situation of imperfect competition. They try to differentiate their products in order to gain and retain market share. However, they have to communicate to consumers that their products are different and better than their competitors. They have to invest in advertising their products.

Advertising is one of the factors that influence demand and is designed to shift demand curve to the right (increase in demand with associated increase in the quantities demanded). Most of the goods now have become commodities. It is difficult for customers to differentiate between say one cars from another within the same price range. Under these circumstances firms have to advertise in order to persuade consumers that their products are preferable to those of their competitors.

There are two kinds of advertisement. The first kind gives consumer's information about their products or services without attempting to persuade. For example, when a circus comes to the town they advertise to inform people about what it entails, where and when it is going to take place and the cost of entry.

The second kind of advertisement is undertaken with a sole purpose to persuade consumer to buy their products. These days there are numerous amount of advertising about reducing wrinkles; these are 'stop ageing' products. Manufacturers of these products go out of their way to 'inform' consumers why their products are better as a result of various so-called scientific tests and the bottom line is to get the consumers to change their attitude and to buy their products.

Advertising can affect the price elasticity of a product or service. If advertising is successful, the price elasticity of demand may fall which then gives a producer an opportunity to increase the price to recover its advertising costs. In this situation his sales will increase.

Marketing perspective

Advertising includes persuasive or information messages carried by a mass medium such as newspaper or television. Advertising works well when there is a need to inform or persuade many people very quickly or when there is a need to address multi-segment market. Some advertising involves the use of celebrities and sports personalities.

Advertising can be divided into comparative advertising and general advertising. In comparative advertising, comparisons are made with competitors' products. For example, Tesco compares their products with Sainsbury's or McDonalds comparing their products with Burger King.

General adverting makes no such comparison; it provides information about the attributes of the products or benefits of the products to the consumers.

Globalisation and advertising

1980s was the period of intense competition and the globalisation process was making its mark. The organisations began to view the world market as a triad comprising the regions of Asia-Pacific, the North Americas and Europe. This came about because of intensive international competition. The diffusion of innovation and convergence of technologies also played a key role in accelerating the globalisation process. Such developments meant that organisations now have to consider very seriously the way they communicate with their customers in a borderless world –in the market which had no frontiers. Differences in cultures and the way words were translated had to be considered. Advertisements were being adapted to reflect local (national) cultures.

Coca-Cola and McDonalds images were being portrayed in different countries via print and television advertisements. The Coca Cola advertisement featured common every day folk across the globe –Black, White, Middle Eastern, Asians– beating their own local version of drums to the beat of the Coca Cola jingle.

Globalisation has also prompted many academics and consultants to undertake researches and surveys to understand cultural differences in order to make marketing communication effective.

Studies were being undertaken to examine the impact of sexual imagery in different countries. An exploratory study was undertaken in the UK, Germany and Italy by Paushali Lass and Susan Hart (83) towards sexual imagery in alcohol advertising. The study was conducted among consumers aged between 18 and 35 in the United Kingdom, Germany and Italy. Results indicated that Italians overall have higher acceptance levels towards sexual imagery portrayed in advertisements as compared to German and British consumers. Furthermore, varying levels of sexual imagery are much more appealing to men than women in all three countries. Consumers' values and lifestyles also played an important role in their overall perception. Moral values in particular are an indicator of acceptance levels of sexual content.

Some researchers were looking at the effect of comparative advertising in communicating product superiority to consumers across different cultures. Comparative advertising involves comparing one product brand against another product brand, examples being Coca Cola v. Pepsi or McDonalds v. Burger King. It has been found that in countries like the USA comparative advertising that highlights the superiority of the target brand is seen as more effective. In some countries such as Thailand, comparative advertising was not as effective. Marketing communication, therefore, has to consider the fact that consumers behave differently to marketing stimuli across cultures.

Understanding cultural differences is, therefore, a must for successful international advertising. Consumers respond to advertising according to their values and the way they have brought up in their societies. Advertising messages have to be congruent with their culture.

Experts are still debating whether standardised approach to advertising at global level is more effective than adapted or specialised approach to advertising where differences in cultures are accommodated.

Theodore Levitt wrote another ground-breaking article on 'the Globalisation of markets. In it he put forward a view that needs and desires of consumers around the world are growing and becoming more homogenized. The world is becoming one large global market. This meant that advertisers can adopt standardised approach in conveying similar messages.

The standardised v. specialised (local) debate picked up tremendous momentum after the publication of Levitt's article. Today different types of advertising are being used by companies like Unilever, Shell, Coca Cola and McDonalds to gain foothold in the global market. These organisations have adopted 'global localisation' strategies as opposed to pure standardised strategy in formulating their marketing mix. Global localisation means '**thinking globally and acting locally**.' Acting locally in marketing communication perspective involves adopting its sales promotion to accommodate local differences.

Apart from considering cultural differences and family values in different cultures, debates are also taking place the way marketing communication is targeted to children as such. These advertisements relate to products such as candies, clothes, shoes and toys. It is estimated that in the USA alone almost one billion dollars have spent in 2005 on children's television advertising. As cable and satellite television are becoming increasingly available in many countries the amount spent on children advertising will run into billions of US dollars.

Experts on advertising are now taking into consideration family values and parental attitudes across international borders in segmenting their communication patterns.

For marketers it is very important to understand the process of communication and the power of individual perception. Understanding this process will enable marketers   to design advertising campaigns and other promotional campaigns more effectively.

Communication models

Basically there are two models of communication. One is called the **information theory model** and the other one is **the constructivist model**.

The information theory model. In this model, communication is seen as linear process in which a sender formulates a message, then transmits this message over a channel to a receiver.

Some experts refer this model as 'who says what to whom and how' method of communication.

The sender formulates the message in a form of words or pictures or drawings. The sender can be the organisation, or the advertising agencies, or the company spokesman or spokeswoman. This process of translating the message is referred to as encoding. This is very important step as one has to consider the fact the words or the pictures translate exactly what is intended. For example, in designing questionnaires to conduct market research the way questions are phrased and the language used become very important. If it is not done properly then the response in a form of feedback will have no significance. See diagram nine below.

Chapter nine. Diagram 7. Method of communication.

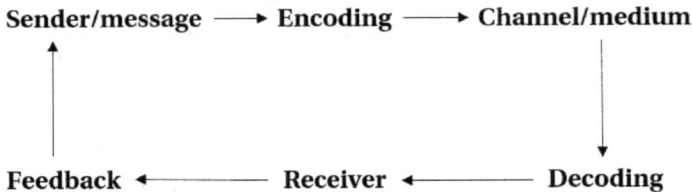

Sender/message ⟶ Encoding ⟶ Channel/medium

Feedback ⟵ Receiver ⟵ Decoding

The channel of communication used could be telephone or e-mails, digital media or face-to-face meetings. The receiver interprets the message (decoding). The interpretation depends on how effective the message is formulated and the biases of the receiver. The message can also be distorted along the channel. In order to compensate for distortion, the sender may formulate the message to include more than is necessary to convey the intent. This is what is referred as 'redundancy' of the message.

In the transactions that take place, the receiver considers and examines the message and provides feedback to sender. This could be in form of purchase or non-purchase. Companies need to put systems in place to monitor feedback.

Information theory has made a large contribution to the development of the various technical systems that we use in communication, such as the telephone, television and computer networks. Nowadays most advertisements are also placed on websites. Understanding of the communication process becomes very helpful.

In designing customer surveys or conducting market research, feedback in a form of response rate becomes very crucial. Marketers have to interpret and evaluate feedback to find out if message is getting through. Unless this is done properly companies will be wasting their marketing budgets.

This type of information system also incorporates an element of 'noise.' Noise introduces distortions in communication system. In marketing sense 'noise' is overexposure of communication. When consumers are bombarded with advertising or direct-mail they switch off and they do not take in messages. Noise also comes about when consumers to whom the advertising is directed are disturbed while watching advertisements.

The biggest drawback of the information theory model is that it assumes that the message is the communication and that it does not take into consideration individual and cultural differences.

The Constructivist Model

We, as individuals, construct mental images and models in order to make sense of our environment. This model assumes that individuals are not the same. They are different in terms of their personalities and thinking patterns and that these differences influence the way they receive information and the way they interpret information.

If communication is presented to us in a form of words, first we try to put all the words together in a way that becomes meaningful to use. How we interpret the words depend on the way we have brought up to write and speak and the language we use. This is why it is very important to understand that we do not simply translate words to communicate to different customers in different countries. How the words are interpreted will depend on the whole social context of the countries involved or targeted.

At individual level our brain has the capacity to reassemble words and images into a meaningful one. For example, if you look at the following image, our brain screens the image and then reassembles all the dots into a meaningful image –a dog– or so we think.

Following is diagram eight of chapter nine.

Chapter nine. Diagram 8. An image.

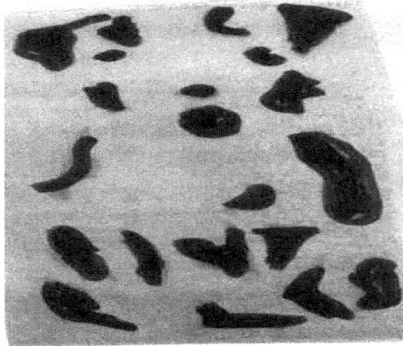

In 1990, the author of this book was delivering communication programme to a group of managers in Jeddah in United Arab Republic. In explaining the process of perception, the writer used the same image (as above) and asked the participants to say what they saw. To his amazement 29 out of 31 participants did not identify the above image (Image one) as a dog.

The author was told by some participants that a dog is not a welcome animal in an Arab culture. People in such a culture do not keep dogs as pets and they do not see dogs very much and this cultural aspect had an influence the way they interpreted this image. This type of understanding is very important for those trying to communicate images and slogans across cultures.

What customers perceive, customers must receive

The constructivist model says that each person, even within the same culture, *constructs* their understanding according to their experience, education and their upbringing.

Perception involves observation, screening, organisation and interpretation. It is the process we use to make sense out of our environment by selecting, screening, organising and interpreting information from the environment. We then exercise judgement to come to conclusions about our perception.

Different individuals have different socially constructed realities. Unfortunately, in practice and in life there is not just one *correct* version of reality. We, therefore, have to be aware of these differences and segment target audience based on similarities when designing marketing communication.

As indicated before being customer-oriented means **'empathising' with customers** and assuming their mode of thinking behaviour to effectively design marketing communication. Empathising with your customers mean that you start with assuming that there are individual differences then you have to think how you would feel if you were in their situations and what would be your expectations as customers. You have to stop thinking as a marketer and start thinking as a customer. You have to abandon your own mental image of a product as a marketer. We have to take alternative viewpoint or alternative reality on board.

Many marketers do not really understand the importance of empathy and the importance of constructivist method of communication. Conducting market research (assuming that the questions are formulated properly) provides insight into alternative realities. Adopting the customers' world view leads to an understanding and knowledge which can be valuable when we are predicting how customers would respond to a particular message.

A strength of the constructivist model is that it constantly reminds us that others may interpret our words, symbols, images etc., differently from how we had intended. Cultural differences also play significant part in translating marketing messages. This view has to be kept in mind especially now when we are dealing with various digital media and platforms.

Consider these- Some marketing disasters from the past few years.

- The company Electrolux, a Scandinavian company that manufactures and sells vacuum cleaners, first attempted to market in the United States in the 1970s. Their chosen slogan was, 'Nothing sucks like an Electrolux'.
- When an American car company GM tried to market its popular Chevy Nova in Latin America, sales were extremely disappointing. They only later realised that the term 'Nova' in Spanish mean 'No Go.'
- American company McDonalds when first opened in Japan, the character Ronald McDonald was introduced, with his usual bright red hair and white painted face. The colour and makeup combination was representative of a death omen in Japanese culture.
- When Pepsi tried to use slogan 'Come alive with Pepsi', in Japan, the translation came to mean, 'Bring back your dead ancestors with Pepsi.'

There are numerous other examples of marketing communication failures as a consequence of poor translation and cultural differences.

Beware of sensitivities involved

One also has to pay attention to certain sensitivities when addressing different segments of the market. For example, since the invasion of Afghanistan and Iraq many Middle Eastern Countries have become anti-Americans and all that America stands for. Coca Cola, for example is associated with promoting Americanism and recently in many Middle Eastern countries demonstrations have taken place to ban Coca Cola. Marketers have to have their ears on the ground not to accentuate such feelings by promoting their products aggressively. We have also seen such an anti-Denmark feeling and boycotting of Danish goods as a result of offending cartoons about Prophet Muhammed published by Danish newspapers.

On March 6, 2007 there was a documentary on British television on Coca Cola showing protests in various countries against Coca Cola Company and boycotting Coca Cola drinks. In India the company was accused of allegedly polluting the environment; in Columbia it was accused of encouraging management by intimidation.

The author has recently read on a situation where one marketing agency was meeting his two clients from the Middle East during the Ramadan month. During the meeting during the day time they offered the clients (who were fasting) tea or coffee!

Mini Case on advertising which takes on board some of the issues raised

Coca Cola

The history of Coca Cola advertising is very fascinating one. The first television advertisement for Coca Cola was created in 1950. The advertising formats included animation, stop motion and live-action ads featuring celebrities like Connie Francis and McGuire Sisters. In 1963, the advertisement carried a slogan 'Things go better with coke'. The slogan had a global appeal which meant that in can be translated into any language and still command that appeal.

Throughout the 1960s Coca Cola experimented with different types of advertisement within the television medium and changing the slogans to reflect the changing times. The most successful television advertisement campaigns were the 'Hilltop commercial' featuring the song 'I'd like to Buy the World a Coke.'

Various advertisement campaigns since then were accompanied with different slogans to reflect the themes of the time. The main objective of the slogans was to depict reliability, happiness, and reward associated with drinking coke. In early 1982, Coca Cola launched a new advertising campaign 'Coke Is It!' with an emphasis on the product's qualities of taste and refreshment.

Over the years the advertising campaigns used a variety of approaches including humour, music, stories, animation to appeal to global audience.

The interesting aspect of Coca Cola advertising campaigns is its understanding of cultural differences and capitalising on these differences to promote its products. In 1998, for example for the Muslim fasting month of Ramadan, the commercial was titled 'Charity.' This campaign ran in twenty Muslim countries.

In the ad, a young boy and his mother bring small gifts to an orphanage: the mother gives a rug and basket of food and the boy donates a bottle of Coca-Cola. At the orphanage, the boy plays football with some of the orphans and makes friends with them. Later, after the breaking of the fast, the boy scampers back to the orphanage to break fast—and share the Coca-Cola—with his new-found friends. The commercial ends with the words "Always in good spirit. Always Coca-Cola."

The constructivist model of communication draws our attention to various factors such as socialisation, our background, our lifestyles, our income, our language, our socio-economic groups and above all our values that affect the way we filter communication messages.

There is some interesting information on "International Marketing: *Why Cultural Awareness Is Important*" an article written by Rajiv Sighamony (84). He provided good examples on taking into consideration cultural issues in advertising and product specifications.

Digital advertising

According to Lin Pophal:

"While there are a wide range of digital advertising trends impacting content marketers, there are a few that rise to the top as those to be most focused on in 2014, according to those who have already actively embraced digital advertising and are attuned to the digital landscape. They include the following trends:

- *Big Data*
- *Location-based communications*
- *Depth of content*
- *Micro video*
- *Mobile*
- *Multiplatform consumption*
- *Personalization"* (85)

These trends provide ability to gather and measure data and from information promote creation of marketing knowledge. Consumers also get information on mobile devices and video clips and marketing content is delivered effectively and efficiently.

In his recent interview which took place in January, 2016 on the *'Future of Marketing,'* (86) Philip Kotler stated the importance of Digital marketing and identified the use of the Internet of Things, Artificial Intelligence, Mobile Marketing and Neural scanning used in marketing operations and activities.

One aspect that should be mentioned within the context of digitisation is The Internet of Things (IoT).

The Internet of Things is starting to bring interconnectivity into the homes of consumers. **IoT** is connecting any device to the internet. The experts tell us the relationship will be between people-people, people-things and things-things. According to Gartner Inc. there will be nearly 26 billion- devices on the internet of things by

2020. Digitisation as we are experiencing it now will multiply and enhance the benefits of connectivity.

In 2016, Marketo, a marketing automation vendor published very useful information on The Internet of Things, specifically on "The Marketing Power of the Internet of Things connectivity for customer better interactivity. According to the information provided

> *"51% of the world's top global marketers expect IoT will revolutionize the marketing landscape by 2020."* (87)

Jamshed Dubash writing in Marketing Journal in January, 2016 on *"Marketing and the Internet of Things: are you ready?"* (88) wrote very useful and interesting information on the impact of the Internet of Things on marketing.

Most of the websites now provided by organisations like PwC, KPMG, Gartner Inc. and so on explain fully the impact of digitisation on well- being of societies. Marketers have to keep ahead acquiring information and converting this experience into knowledge in order to perform their tasks efficiently and effectively. In digital world marketers have to turn themselves into "smart" marketers.

Finally, it is very important to deliver what is being advertised. Do not make promises if you cannot deliver.

Always remember to deliver what you are communicating.

Let me tell you a story:

> *"A tiger met a lion as they drank beside the pool.*
> *'Tell me' said the tiger, 'why are you always roaring like a fool.'*
> *'It's not so foolish', said the lion with a twinkle in his eyes.*
> *'They call me King of Beasts; it pays to advertise.'*
> *A little rabbit overheard, and ran home like a streak.*
> *He thought he'd try the lion's plan but his roar was just a squeak.*
> *And a hungry fox that morning had his breakfast in the woods."*

The moral: it does not pay to advertise unless you can deliver the good. Anon (89).

Promotion

Besides advertising firms also engage in other promotional media.

Direct selling is done either by print – direct mail to customers or direct call (cold calling) to customers or door-to-door selling or open market selling. Some direct selling is 'hard sell' where the person selling is presenting the product/service very aggressively as is the case with some insurance salesmen and saleswomen. 'Soft sell' involves subtle approach adopted by sales people. They might say "we are not selling anything but we happen to be in your area should you want to consider double glazing!"

Exhibitions and fairs are used by car manufacturers, boats manufacturers, and computers and even by service providers such as Business Schools (MBA fair) to promote the products and services.

Branding involves giving an identity to product or an organisation. The practice of branding goes back hundreds of years where certain products were associated with certain regions. For example, cloth of Arras, Bordeaux wine, Sheffield steel and so on. The main objective of branding is to build an image of a product or a company and to convey this image with what it stands for to the consumers.

Brand communicates attributes (speed, quality, durability), benefits (comfort, safety), personality (matching the desired self-image of buyers with the brand's image) and values.

Consumers establish a set of beliefs about a particular brand. These beliefs are based on perceptions, which in turn create expectations. What organisations have to do is to manage these expectations.

Public Relations. According to the Institute of Public Relations, it is 'deliberate, *planned and sustained effort to establish and maintain mutual understanding between an organisation and its public.'*

Companies engage in public relations in order to create and sustain its image among customers and key groups in a society such as politicians, educations and so on.

One of the examples of public relations initiative was that practised by McDonalds. In conjunction with the 2006 Winter Games in Torino, Italy, McDonald's Corporation officially launched the global rollout of the Nutrition Information Initiative, which will provide consumers with nutrition information on product packaging.

Caution: Public relations can also harm your company and your products. In February, 1990 Perrier Group of America Inc., the U.S. unit of France's Source Perrier S.A. announced a highly embarrassing product recall. Recall was made because the Perrier bottled-water was contaminated with benzene, a poisonous liquid shown to cause cancer in laboratory animals.

The incident turned into public disaster because the company's explanation for the recall kept changing. There were numerous statements made which contradicted with one another. These inconsistent statements raised consumers' suspicions. This recall came at a time when Perrier was experiencing very intense competition from its competitors.

What is the difference between PR and advertising? Robert Wynne writing in Forbes in July 2014 stated:

"A recent study from 2014 by Nielsen commissioned by in Powered on the role of content in the consumer decision-making process concluded that PR is almost 90% more effective than advertising: "On average, expert content lifted familiarity 88 percent more than branded content..." but I think that's low. With advertising, you tell people how great you are. With publicity, others sing your praises. Which do you think is more effective?" (90)

Public Relations are one of the marketing communication tools which are advocated by marketing experts in the new economy.

These tools have the capacity to adapt its message according to consumers' value.

Philanthropy

This normally would be categorised as marketing communication but according to the writer philanthropic giving is similar to public relations. Whatever the motive for giving, the act of giving enhances the image of the corporation in the eyes of the community. It is a form of corporate communication marketing its corporate values and mission.

Not long ago Bill Gates the founder of Microsoft has given in the region of $ 40 billion to tackle health and poverty problems in different countries. He is not the only 'philanthrocapitalist' according to the Economist, (91) Pierre Omidyar, the founder of e-Bay, Sergey Brin and Larry page, the founders of Google, Gordon Moore, Intel's co-founder, Anita Roddick, founder of the Body Shop and others are making contributions to improve the status of the disadvantaged sectors of the world community.

In an article written by Doug Conant in September, 2013 by McKinsey & Company *"Why Philanthropy is R&D for Business"* (92), examples are given on how Campbell Soup company, Vodafone and IBM aremaking various philanthropic initiates.

Packaging

A package is an extension of the product offered for sale. It provides information to buyers regarding products and also conveys product benefits. Consumers now are demanding information on the ingredients of the product and their health benefits and they are expecting manufacturers to provide the information on the packaging.

McDonalds, for example, have announced that they were now going to communicate nutrition information to its customers around the world. The new package will be rolled out beginning in the first half of 2006 in restaurants in North America, Europe, Asia and Latin America. By the end of 2006, McDonalds plans to have nutrition information featured on packaging in more than 20,000 of its restaurants.

They say customer input led the decision to implement the programme. Tests were conducted in Colombia, Hong Kong, Scotland, Shanghai, Spain and the USA. The results indicated that the customers liked the approach.

Dell computers use a clever technique to involve consumers in purchasing decision. To buy Dell computer on-line you are given the facility to configure your own computer making decision on the type of memory you want, the type of processor, monitor and so on.

Note on product manuals

When you buy appliances you have manuals to explain the operating mode of the appliance in question and it is supposed to be user-friendly. But judging by comments from numerous customer's manuals are not written with customers in mind. They are in many cases incoherent and confusing. This is so even in cases of digitised manuals.

Some marketers have informed me that manuals do not form part of marketing communication. Therefore, it is not appropriate to pay attention to manuals. The writer is given to understand by some electrical appliances sellers that significant proportion of appliances is returned because customers cannot understand or follow operating manuals. Also 'words of mouth' is very powerful force to stop people buying those products. It is, therefore, important to pay attention to product manuals and consider them as a component of marketing communication.

Sponsorships: Many companies sponsor activities in order to establish relationships with partners and individuals. Sponsors get in return rights and association that may be used to gain commercial advantage.

Sports sponsorships are becoming increasingly popular as promotional tool for sports and non-sports products.

Many companies such as Gillette, Toyota, Royal Bank of Scotland, Nike and so on sponsor sports and other activities in order to promote products as well as promote their corporate image. Companies now also sponsor television plays and reality shows.

In many cases sponsorships and public relations go hand by hand.

Toshiba has sponsored the Science Museum in London since 1997. The Science Museum has the most sophisticated navigational aids for visitors and the terminals display information about the museum in several languages.

Product placement

This is a form of advertising but it is done in a very subtle way. Product placement involves obtaining screen time (television and cinemas) for consumer products such as cars, computers, food and so on. We are told that Apple Computers paid a lot of money to get Tom Cruise to use Apple Computer in the film 'Mission Impossible.' We often see examples of cars, plane, clothes, sun glassed with specific brands used in the film or television clips to grab our attention in a subliminal way. Psychologists tell us that visual impact is far more powerful than verbal impact. Some visual advertisement is symbolic in that they represent importance and aspirations.

All the above communication tools can be used either dependently or concurrently. The object of marketing mix is to create awareness, interest, desire and action – **A. I. D. A. Principle**: Make customers first aware of want is available, then capture their interest by highlighting the benefits of the product or service to them and what the attributes of the product are, get them to think about acquiring this product and finally make them to commit to buying the product.

Note on marketing mix

As every student of marketing knows product mix is the key ingredient of marketing process. The mix consists of product, price, place and promotion. Marketers now argue the components of 'mix' are looked at from producers' perspective. In the age of marketing where focus is on customers the components of marketing mix should be cost, customer benefits, convenience, communication and customer engagement.

Chapter Ten
Economics of Customers

Importance of customers

Customers in the modern economy are considered to be part of the production process; they are in fact one of the key factors of production. Dell customers can order computers directly from Dell and they are given the facility to design their own computers. Rover customers can order a 'made-to-measure' car, in effect, straight from the factory. With the multimedia system, customers can browse through an electronic catalogue of all available models within a specified price range. Or, if they already know what they want, they can follow the build-in-order approach.

Supply and demand, though still important levers in price mechanism, cease to be mutually exclusive as presented in economics. The inter-relationship between demand and supply has become very complicated and diffused as a result of accelerated technological development and digitisation of various markets involved.

Since 1950s late Peter Drucker (1955) has been writing about the importance of customers to any business. In his book '*The Practice of Management*' he wrote how important for any business is to meet customer satisfaction. A business should have a look from outside in the way customers perceive it to be. It is there to consider customer demand and to meet customer satisfaction. Meeting customer's need and giving customer opportunity to satisfy his or her demand should be one of the key strategic objectives of any business.

Economically and in Marketing, it pays to establish relationship with customers. Many firms now devise different methods of establishing relationship with their customers.

Relationship Marketing

The term relationship marketing came into use to show new emphasis on retaining customers by building commitment in a way of providing excellent customer service and keeping in touch with them via direct communication.

Philip Kotler, the leading marketing guru categorised customer relationship into five types of relationship. They are:

1. **The Basic relationship:** This type of relationship involves selling and buying and there is no further contact.
2. **The Reactive relationship:** This involves selling and buying but customers are encouraged to get in contact if more information is required.
3. **The accountable relationship:** This involves selling and buying but the seller communicates with the customers after the purchase is made to find out if the customer is satisfied with the purchase.
4. **The proactive relationship:** This involves communicating with existing customers to inform them of improvement made in the products or service.
5. **The Partnership relationship:** This involves continuous contact with the customer with a view to bringing about customer savings.

Relationship marketing involves building satisfying relationship with various key stakeholders including customers, employees, distributors, agencies, governments and different types of partners involved to build effective marketing networks.

The 1970s witnessed the accelerated development of service sector and the emergence of service marketing. This development prompted paradigm shift from transactions to relationships.

Relationship marketing attempts to involve and integrate customers, suppliers and other partners into company's developmental and marketing activities. It reflects interdependence rather than independence of choice among partners.

The growth of relationship marketing can be attributed to the rapid technological advancements, the adoption of total quality initiatives by some companies, accelerated growth of service sector and an increase in competitive pressure.

According to some marketing experts, the recognition that customer retention was central to service marketing focused attention on the notion of creating service relationships. Relationships necessarily involve targeted individualised communication as opposed to communication directed at mass market.

According to Michael Baker, (93) the emphasis is now put on Customer Relationship Marketing (CRM) and Customer Relationship Management (CRM). CRM, according to Baker, is a technology tool which enables an organisation to integrate various database systems in order to focus on customer.

However, some companies are finding out that their investment in CRM is not bringing marketing returns. This may be due to the fact that to become market-oriented and to reap the benefits of CRM there has to be a change in organisation culture. The mind-set of an organisation has to shift from becoming sales-driven or production-driven to marketing driven mentality. Every employee in the organisation has to think and act as marketer in order for CRM to become profitable. CRM is not about getting the right software or the right technology; it is about assuming marketing mind-set.

The value of investing in long term relationships with customers varies with the type of business. For example, service organisations like consultants, financial institutions and lawyers would definitely benefit from instituting CRM. Dell Computer and IBM have shown also that proper management of CRM bears good returns. Their CRM process involves co-operation from consumers. It is this type of involvement and collaboration which is now advocated by marketing gurus and marketing experts. Those who exclude consumers in their marketing do so at their own peril.

Big Data is now being integrated into organisation CRM solution. This integration enables organisations to focus effectively on customers' expectations and improve customer service delivery. Big data in conjunction with CRM can be used by all kind of organisations, big and small.

Relationship Life Cycle model

Relationship between organisations and customers (B2C) and organisations to organisations (B2B) go through lifecycle before it culminates into long-term sustained relationship. Different writers and marketing gurus have presented different stages of relationship development. Generally speaking, there are the following four stages:

1. The discovery stage

At this stage the organisation is identifying suitable customer to do business with. Once interest is created in a specific customer/ client, the organisation then starts to build database on that customer/client. This database would capture information on the needs, attributes, and expectations of the customer. This is essentially an information gathering stage.

2. The development stage

At this stage the organisation begins to target this customer/client with well-designed marketing mix and communications mix tools. Together with offering core services based on needs of the customer, the organisation is also promoting supporting and enhanced services to catch the interest of the customer/client.

3. The commitment stage

At this stage the customer/client experience the product/service purchased and delivered. At this stage the assessment of the quality, customer service, after-sales service and communication takes place. If satisfied on all counts commitment is made for repeat exchanges. Through repeat exchanges relationship begins to develop and trust begins to build.

The organisation also commits itself to meet changing customer/client needs and to keep abreast with technological developments.

4. The loyalty stage

At this stage solid relationship is developed and value is created by both parties and there is mutual interdependence. The two parties are working together to deliver value.

Theodore Levitt (1986) (94) compares the relationship between the organisation and its customer like that of man and woman bound by marital contract. He felt the relationship between a customer and a seller will remain good only if the relationship is managed effectively.

This type of relationship can also be compared to a romantic relationship. In the early stages 'A' is looking to establish relationship with, B, 'A' begins to search for a romantic partner and identifies 'B' as potential partner.

In the next stage 'A' begins to find out more about 'B' and makes an approach. 'B' also begins to develop interest and finds out about how 'A' can meet his/her needs and expectations.

Information gathering stage comes to an end and courting begins. The courting then deepens and the couple gets engaged thus indicating their willingness to enter into commitment.

The next stage the parties declare their commitment and get married. At this stage parties trust each and other and there is a deep relationship.

Both parties have to work hard by being open with each other and trusting each other to sustain this relationship on a long term

basis. As time passes needs and expectations change and both parties, if they have to avoid divorce have to meet each other's needs.

Economics of customer retention and loyalty

Customer loyalty describes the tendency of a customer to choose
one business or product over another for a particular need. In non-
generic industries, customers may be described as being "brand
loyal" because they tend to choose a certain brand more often than
others. Customers may express high satisfaction levels with an organisation In a survey, but satisfaction does not equal loyalty. Loyalty is demonstrated by the actions of the customer – customers can
be very satisfied and still not be loyal. Customer loyalty has become
a catch-all term for the end result of many marketing approaches
where customer data is used. Customer loyalty can be improved by
well-managed customer retention programmes, and customers
who are targeted by these demonstrate higher loyalty to an organisation. All customer retention programmes rely on communicating
with customers, giving them encouragement to remain active, and
choosing to do business with a company. Reichheld (1996) refers to
loyalty as *"the litmus test of corporate Performance."* An important
marketing measure of customer loyalty is the degree of "churn" in
the customer base.

Customer Loyalty Ladder

According to Payne, (1996):

> *"Customers can be characterised by their degree of loyalty:
> 'hardcore loyal' (who buy from the company all the time); 'soft-
> core loyals (who are loyal most of the time; 'shifting loy-*

als'(who will shift between the company and another competitor). And 'switchers' (who show little loyalty towards any supplier or service." (95)

Payne, Adrian (1994) (96) also in explaining how relationship with customers can be managed and sustained presented the customer loyalty ladder model.

The first step on the ladder is a **prospect**. He/she is someone whom you believe may be persuaded to do business with you. The main challenge here is to attract prospect and convert him/her into a customer.

A customer is someone who has done business once with your organisation. The main task for marketers here is to get this customer to do repeat business with your organisation. According to Payne, organisations make little efforts to get customers to do repeat business and convert them into client. Most of the efforts go towards winning new customers rather than improving relationship with existing customer and moving them up the ladder.

A client is someone who does repeat business with your organisation but is not loyal to your organisation. Repeat business does not equate loyalty.

A client has to be transformed into **a supporter**. A supporter is positively disposed towards your organisation but the support is passive. There is no active engagement with your organisation.

Efforts should be put to convert a supporter into **an advocate**. An advocate is very pleased with your service and actively recommends your service or products to others. Word of mouth and referral through advocates bring new business and new customers.

Finally, an advocate should be converted to **a partner** who has a close and long term relationship with your organisation. At this stage the customer trusts the company.

Relationship marketing loyalty ladder can also be applied to internal customers mainly employees. Organisations can make efforts to devote resources in developing and training their employees and to convert employees into partners.

Reichheld Service Profit Cycle

A loyal customer can be a consistent source of revenue over a period of years. Reichheld and Sasser (97) popularised the term **'zero defections'** which they describe as keeping every customer the company can serve profitably.

Reichhelld and Sasser undertook an analysis of profit per customer in a various service business. They found out that there was a direct relationship between the volume of profit and the number of years the customers dealt with the businesses. The longer they stayed with businesses the more profits they generated.

Stages by which loyal customers enhance profits:

- Existing customers over time purchase more quantities as a result of changing circumstances such as the growth in their families and or becoming more affluent. Thus enhancing revenue.
- As customers become more experienced they make less demands on businesses thus enhancing business productivity by reducing operating costs.
- These customers recommend organisations that serve them well to others thus generating new customers. More revenues accrue to the businesses.
- Highly satisfied customers are willing to pay premium prices.

What keeps customers loyal is the value they receive. According to Reichheld,

"Although some executives do realise that profits are really a downstream benefit of delivering superior value to customers-and that customer loyalty is therefore the best indicator of strategic success or failure they lack the tools they need to focus their organizational learning on this most basic building block of profitable growth." (98)

It is however, important that loyal customers are treated well. When Apple dropped the price of iPhone by a third after only two months in the market, customers who were loyal to Apple complained bitterly. Steve Jobs, Chief Executive Office of Apple apologised and offered partial rebate.

Why are loyal customers more profitable?

In general, the key benefits of retaining a customer include:

- It is three to ten times cheaper to sell to existing customers than to new ones,
- even a small increase in customer loyalty can result in a large increase in profitability,
- return on investment is higher as your marketing is better targeted, and
- you are better able to find new customers when you take the opportunity to understand loyal ones.

Bear in mind that industries will differ, for example acquisition costs may be high for a mortgage company, but low for the fast-moving consumer goods (FMCG) sector. Referral rates of new customers by existing ones may diminish over time as the novelty of a new product or service wears off.

Acquisition cost

Acquisition cost is the cost of getting a new customer. This may be in advertising, personal selling, direct mail, the expense of opening a new shop, time invested in writing a proposal or making a pitch and so on. Some of these costs are obvious and some are hidden. The important thing is to make sure that an objective and realistic figure is gained of all the costs of gaining a new customer.

Reinartz and Kumar's study (2002) (99) of the relationship between Customer loyalty and profits from 16,000 customers in four Organisations' databases did not find any evidence to support the view that customer loyalty and profitability are linked. What they did find was that the link between customers and profitability was more complicated because customers fall into *four* groups, not two.

Not all loyal customers are profitable, and not all profitable customers are loyal. Traditional tools for segmenting customers do a poor job of identifying that latter group, causing organisations to chase expensively after initially profitable customers who hold little promise of future profits. Reinartz and Kumar suggest an alternative approach, based on well-established "event-history modelling" techniques, that more accurately predict future buying probabilities. Armed with such a tool, marketers can correctly identify which customers belong in which category and market accordingly.

The challenge in managing customers who are profitable but disloyal is to market as aggressively as you can *while they're buying from you.* A "soft" approach is more appropriate for the profitable customers who are likely to stay loyal. As for highly loyal but not very profitable customers, there is a need to find out whether they have the potential to spend more than they currently do. With those customers who generate no loyalty and no profits the answer is simple: identify early and don't invest anything.

Base profit

Customers normally pay a price for a product that is in excess of the costs of producing it. The longer the customer stays with the organisation, the longer it can continue to earn the base profit, which can be used to pay off the initial acquisition costs.

Revenue growth

In most industry sectors, customer spending tends to accelerate over time as customers become more familiar with the brand. For example, as the customer appreciates the range on offer from a retailer, they tend to extend their purchasing across more categories.

A benefit of long-term customer retention is that satisfied customers tend to refer more. The evidence on this is mixed depending on product category. In some categories, customers tend to refer more in the early stages of the buying relationship when novelty encourages word-of-mouth, e.g. dentists. Long-standing customers pay higher prices than new ones. They do not benefit from introductory offers or discounts and tend not to be as price sensitive.

Measuring the economic value of the customer to the organisation (EVCO)

Day and Fahey (1988) (100) have examined ways of calculating the value of loyal customers by calculating the economic value of the customer to the organisation (EVCO). There are two approaches to calculating the EVCO. The management accounting approach uses customer profitability analysis, which is a form of activity-based costing, whilst the *marketing* approach prefers to use customer lifetime valuation, which is a type of discounted cash flow analysis.

Using activity-based costing to calculate EVCO

Some customers are more profitable than others. In the past accountants have calculated EVCO in an approximate way by determining customer profitability through an allocating a commensurate proportion of operating costs. For example, if a particular customer generated 20 per cent of total sales revenue, then 20 per cent of costs were allocated against the gross margin generated by that customer. Such *pro rata* allocations are insensitive to the actual level of service-oriented resources that a customer consumes. Customer profitability analysis (CPA) uses activity-based costing to attribute differences in customer profitability to differences in the ways in which customers or segments consume resources. In particular, CPA seeks to trace and cost customer-driven activities, such as purchasing, delivery, accounting and inventory management to measure EVCO more accurately. When CPA is adopted, EVCO is measured in two stages.

First of all, the costs are assigned to products. Customers who purchase high-cost products are charged properly by applying the costs against the customer's product mix. The second step is to assign to the customer the expenses and assets that are driven by the sale and marketing process. The result is the total cost associated with a customer. This cost is compared with the customer's revenue stream to establish their true profitability.

Using discounted cash flow analysis to calculate EVCO

Customer lifetime analysis (CLV) measures the present value of the future net cash flows expected to be received over the lifetime of a customer relationship. Four general steps are followed to calculate CLV:

(1) customers or segments are identified.

(2) their current profitability is assessed.

(3) current profitability is projected to estimate future cash flows.

(4) expected cash flows are discounted over an organisation's planning horizon to arrive at their net present value.

Customers and segments that generate a positive net present value are considered to be economically valuable.

Whichever way we look at customers, without them there is no business and without business there is no marketing.

There is an interesting article on Economic value of the Customer entitled "*A Refresher on the Economic Value to the Customer*" written by Amy Gallo in the *Harvard Business Review* of 07, May, 2015 (101) in which she explains the concept of EVC and the mistakes some managers make in calculating EVC.

In conventional as well as in digital marketing, focus on customers and understanding their expectations and meeting their needs and requirements becomes the most important issue. Personalisation becomes very important in winning customer loyalty and gaining customer retention. Digital technology is moving fast and it is enabling marketers to creating meaningful customer journeys.

A good example of personalising customer experience is the use of British Gas Hive. The author's friend has an app and through this app called Hive he is able to control his heating and adjust his settings does not matter where he is. He is very happy with this experience and seems happy in relation to his customer journey with British Gas.

The obvious outcomes of this include much improved customer service levels, better customer retention, higher conversion rates and an improved overall customer lifetime value. Alongside this, building a complete and personalised picture of each customer and their journey can generate insight that guides customer experience improvement programmes. Customer data becomes very important in creating personalization. Big data needs to be restructured to interact with customers. Organisations like Amazon, Google and Apple do very well to create customer data.

Circular Economy

In relation to consumers, the author would like to conclude by referring to the following three highlights of the article on "*What the Circular Economy Means to Marketers.*"

1. "*We will need to change how we think about many of the basic concepts marketers deal with every day: concepts such as identity and desire, loyalty and reward, and trust and transparency. These changes represent an opportunity to reinvent the role of marketing.*"
2. *While the marketer-customer relationship will change, so too will loyalty and reward schemes, shifting from cross-*

selling and upselling to rewards for being suppliers of insight, advice, recommendation and raw materials.

3. *"It's important to educate customers about quality and value, and show them the benefits of re-marketed products such as re-furbished or re-manufactured products."* (102)

Focus on customers, in terms of customer engagement and customer loyalty, becomes the key point of marketing and also the key point of economics in terms of customers wanting to make appropriate choice.

Conclusion

We have seen throughout these ten chapters that economics is about allocation of scare resources based on demand and supply. Demand in economics is effective demand, that is, demand backed by money or purchasing power. It is not easy to influence demand by price mechanism alone. Firms have to understand needs of consumers and produce goods that meet their needs. However, the business world has changed dramatically over the last three decades and the competition is becoming very intensive nationally and internationally. Firms need to reach consumers and to do so they have to devise effective communication techniques in order to capture the market share. This is where marketing merge with economics and technological developments play key role.

Digitisation process also has significantly affected and is affecting the way marketers communicate with consumers and consumers with marketers. Various media in digitisation process are constantly changing and as consequence marketers have to be on alert on various developments taking place so that communication can be taken place in real time. According to a new McKinsey Global Institute (MGI) report, *Digital globalization: 'The new era of global flows,'* (103) we now have to pay attention to soaring flows of data and information in relation to Digital Globalisation.

The foundation of marketing is economics. Economic principles can be applied and adapted to capture and penetrate market share. Marketers have to understand the nature of economics. Economists, in turn, have to understand the economics of customers and haw global process and the modern economy are making some economic principles redundant and in many cases diffusing key concepts such as demand and supply. Consideration also has to be given to the Circular Economy and its impact on marketing. Economics and Marketing has to be studied together and have to come together to make economics more meaningful to those interested in economics; coming together is creating a marriage of necessity.

According to Aside Williams (2015):

"The proliferation of cloud-based CRM tools, sales manage-ment tools, social media tools and cloud marketing software has revolutionised the way businesses can now engage with customers. At the same time, customers now expect a more per-sonalised, tailored real-time experience. This was also further highlighted recently by The Economist Intelligence Unit re-port, where 50 per cent of respondents revealed evolving cus-tomer needs and expectations was the top driver of digital transformation in their business." (104)

The end result today is therefore **customer engagement** and in conventional as well as in digital marketing, executives should focus on this engagement. This is now the theme of the global business world. Organisations have to align their organisational strategy, strategic marketing plan in order to move forward in the world of digitisation and globalisation.

"No great improvements in the lot of mankind are possible until a great change takes place in the fundamental consti-tution of their modes of thought."

John Stuart Mill

References and sources

1. 'Egalitarian as a Revolt Against Nature and Other Essays (Auburn, Alsa: Mises Institute, 2000) p 202. Reprinted by permission from Mises Institute.

2. http://www.wrap.org.uk/content/wrap-and-circular-. Accessed on 14th. February, 2016.economy?
    gelid=CNa5uemG8soCFQccGwod5loFfw

3. http://www.theguardian.com/sustainable-business/10-things-need-to-know-circular-economy. Accessed on 1st. February, 2016.

4. http://etalks.me/philip-kotler-marketing-for better world/. Accessed on 10th. January, 2015.

5. http://www.marketingjournal.org/future-of-marketing-an-interview-with-philip-kotler/. Accessed on 5th. February, 2016.

6. The Economist Newspaper. January 10-16, 2015. UK.

7. Weisman, D. L. and Kulick, R. B. (2010) "Price discrimination, two sided markets, and net neutrality regulation." Tulane Journal of Technology and Intellectual Property, Vol. 13 No. 1. Pp 81-106.

8. Kimes, S. E. and Wirtz, J (2003) "Has revenue management become acceptable? Findings from an international study on the perceived fairness of rate fences." Journal of Service Research, vol.6 No. 2 pp 125-135.

9. Kotler, Philip and Keller, Kevin Lane (2009). "Marketing Management: Analysis, Planning, Implementation and Control. 12th. Ed. ©reprinted by permission of Pearson Education, Inc., New York, New York.

10. http://www.fairtrade.org.uk. Accessed on 26th January, 2016.

11. http://fairtrade.org.uk. Accessed on 26th. January, 2016.

12. Wilson, Alan (2003). 'Marketing Research: An integrated approach" FT/Prentice Hall. 2nd edition also published in 2006.

13. *http://businesscasestudies.co.uk/kelloggs/new-products-from-market-research/why-carry-out-market-research.html l#axzz3yLYIYkFR. Accessed on 20ᵗʰ. January, 2016.*

14. Jagdish N. Sheth (Guru Interview). *Management First.* 7ᵗʰ. February, 2003.

15. 'Marketing Myopia'. *Harvard Business Review,* July-August, 1960. ©1960 by the President and Fellows of Harvard College: all rights reserved.

16. Ronald Coase (1937). '*The Nature of the Firm*' The Free Press. Published on line 19ᵗʰ. February, 2007. http://onlinelibrarywiley.com. Permission granted by Simon and Schuster.

17. Williamson, Oliver (1985) *'The Economic Institutions of the Capitalism'.* Free Press. Permission granted by Simon and Schuster.

18. *http://www.economist.com/news/special-report/21569575-companies-need-think-more-carefully-about-how-they-off-shore-and-outsource-herd-instinct'. Accessed on 17/01/15.*

19. *http://www.economist.com/news/special-report/21569572-after-decade-sendin-work-across-world-companies-are-rethinking-their-offshoring. Accessed on 17/01/15.*

20. Parasuraman, A, Zeithaml, Valerie, A, Berry, Leonard, L (1985) 'A Conceptual Model of Service Quality and Its Implications for Future Research.' *Journal of Marketing* 49, Fall 1995, pp41-50. See Table 1. Permission from American Management Association.

21. Ibid.

22. Lovelock, C and Wirtz, J (2007). *"Services Marketing People, Technology, Strategy"* Pearson Prentice Hall pp425-427.

23. Doyle, Peter (2001). '*Marketing Management and Strategy'.* Third Edition, FT/Prentice hall. 4ᵗʰ. Edition paperback available

24. *Business week.* 31 August, 1988. Pp 57.

25. Margretta, Joan (1998) 'The power of Virtual Integration: an interview with Dell Computers' Michael Dell' *Harvard Business Review.* 1998@ by the President and Fellows of Harvard College: all rights reserved.

26. *http://www.techword.com/news/ux/pizza-huts-new-app-lets-customers-order-with-their-mind-3589085. Accessed on 20/12/15*

27. *https://www.accenture.com/us-en/insight-why-ceo-needs-digital-vision.aspx. Accessed on 15th January, 2016.*

28. Lovelock, Christopher and Wirtz, Jochen (2007), '*Services Marketing*'. Sixth Edition. Pearson/Prentice Hall. New Jersey. Pp185

29. Johnston, Robert (1996), 'Achieving Focus in Service Organisations'. *The Service Industries Journal,* 16 January, 1996. 10-20.

30. Shostack, Lynn. '*Understand services Through Blueprinting*'. In T. Schwartz et al '*Advances in Service marketing and Management*'. 1992. Greenwich, CT: JAIl Press, 1992. The technique of blueprinting was explained by Lynn Shostack in *Harvard Business Review,* vole 62, No 1, Jan-Feb, 1982, pp 133-136. @ 1982 by the President and Fellows of Harvard College: all rights reserved.

31. Cole, Gerald (2004). '*Management Theory and practice*'. Sixth Edition. Thomson Learning. There is also 2011 paperback edition.

32. Peters, Tom (1994). *The Tom Peters Seminar.* Vintage Books. Pp78-79.

33. Gronroos, Christian (1990) '*Service management and marketing* '. Pearson International.

34. *http://www.oxfordtoday.ox.ac.uk/opinion/future-professions-0. Accessed on 10th February, 2016.*

35. *http://forbesindia.com/article/ckgsb/the-thinker-interview-with=philip-kotler-the-father-of-marketing/36951/2. Accessed on 20/01/15.*

36. *http://www.beatoncapital.com/2015/11/why-digitisation-is-a-net-opportunity-for-professional-services/#sthash.lnuSJTVJ.dpuf. Accessed on 12/01/16*

37. Lovelock, Christopher, and Writz, Jochen. '*Services marketing*'. Sixth Edition. Pearson/ Prentice Hall. pp128.

38. Nagle, Thomas, T (1987). '*The Strategy and tactics of Pricing*'. Prentice Hall, New Jersey, pp175-176.

39. Nagle, Thomas (1983) 'Pricing as Creative marketing'. *Business Horizons*, July-August pp19.

40. Porter, Michael (1985) *'Competitive Advantage'*. The Free press, New York. Pp37-38.

41. Lovelock and Weinberg (1978). Public and Nonprofit marketing comes of Age." In Gerald Zaltman and Thomas V. Bonoma eds. *Review of Marketing*. Chicago. American Marketing Association.

42. Kotler, Philip (1982) *'Marketing for Nonprofit Organisations'*. 2nd. Ed., ©1982.Reprinted by permission of Pearson Education, Inc., New York, New York.

43. *Coopers & Lybrand survey*, 1994.

44. Hammer, Michael and Champy, James (1995) *'Re-engineering the Corporation.'* Nicholas Brealey, UK.

45. Copyright. The W. Edwards Deming Institute. First published in Kermally, Sultan (1996). *'Total Management Thinking'* Butterworth-Heinemann. Reprinted from *'Out of the Crisis'* published by The MIT Press. Permission granted by MIT.

46. Gronroos, Christian (2000). *'Service Management and Marketing'*. 2nd. Edition Wiley, UK.

47. Zeithaml, Valerie, a Parasuraman, A and Berry, Leonard l (1990). *'Delivering Quality service'*. The free Press, New York.

48. Parasuraman, a Zeithaml, Valerie A and Malhotra, Arvind (2005). 'E-S-Qual: A Multiple-item Scale for Assessing Electronic Service Quality', *Journal of Service research*, 7, no.3, pp213-233. W Edwards Deming by permission of MIT and the W. Edwards Deming Institute.

49. Rosenthal, Jim and Wade, Judy (1993). 'How to make Re-engineering really work.' Harvard Business Review, November/December. ©1993 by the President and Fellows of Harvard College: all rights reserved).

50. Lewin, Kurt (1951).' *Field Theory in Social Science'* ed. Dorwin Cartwright. Harper, USA.

51. *http://www.forbes.com/sites/davidcooperstein/2012/07/11/marketing-change-management-like-it-or-not-you-have-to-figure-it-out/. Accessed in November, 2015*

52. *http://www.icaew.com/en/archive/library/subject- gate-ways/business-management/performance-manage-ment/benchmarking/small-business-update/10-ways-to-benchmark-your-business. Accessed on 1ˢᵗ. February, 2016.*

53. *http://www.bain.com/publications/articles/management-tools-and-trends-2013.aspx. Accessed on 31ˢᵗ. January, 2016.*

54. *http://www.camrosh.com/author/pantea/. Accessed on 10ᵗʰ. February, 2016*

55. *https://www.gov.uk/government/publications/benchmarking-uk-competitiveness-in-the-global-economy. Accessed on 31ˢᵗ. January, 2016.*

56. *http://unpan1.un.org/intradoc/groups/public/docu-ments/UN/UNPAN023686.pdf. Accessed on 2ⁿᵈ. February, 2016.*

57. *https://www.capgemini.com/resources/full-report-future-proofing-egovernment-for-a-digital-single-market. Accessed on 28ᵗʰ. January, 2016.*

58. Art.3 (1). Regulation 139/2004, *the European Community Merger Regulation*

59. *http://ec.europa.eu/competition*

60. *http://ec.europa.eu/competition*

61. Mitchell, David and Holmes, Garrick (1996). '*Making acqui-sitions Work*' Research Report. The Economist Intelligence Unit. London

62. *www.thehindubusinessline.com/2007/01/05 stories.* Accessed on 08/07/08

63. Kotler, Philip and Keller, Kevin Lane (2006) 'Pearson/Pren-tice Hall. pp57

64. *Economist Newspaper.* September, 23, 2000.

65. Nonaka, I and Takeuchi H (1995) 'T*he Knowledge-Creating Company: How Japanese Companies Create the Dynamics of Innovation*' Oxford University Press, UK.

66. Nonaka, Ikujiro (1991), 'The Knowledge-creating company', *Harvard Business Review,* November-December, pp96-97. ©1991 by the President and Fellows of Harvard College: all rights reserved.

67. *http://graphics.eiu.com/files/ad_pdfs/tata_knowhow_wp.pdf. Accessed on 2nd. February, 2016.*

68. Pollard, D. (2006) 'Promoting learning transfer: developing SME marketing knowledge in the Dnipropetrovsk oblast, Ukraine', Paper presented at the *33rd Annual Academy of InternationalBusiness (AIB) UK Conference*, April 7–8, Manchester.

69. Kohlbacher, F. (2007) *International Marketing in the 21st Century: A Knowledge-based Approach.*

70. *http://www.imf.org/external/np/speeches/2004/062304.htm. The IMF at 60: Equipped for Today's Challenge? Address to the American Academy. By Anne O. Kruger, First Deputy Managing Director, International Monetary Fund, Berlin, June 23, 2004. Accessed on 13/08/15.*

71. *http://www.wto.org. Accessed on 14/07/15.*

72. *https://www.wto.org/english/news_e/news16_e/stat_28jan16_e.htm. Accessed on 01/02/16.*

73. *http://www.fas.usda.gov/tppolcy/NAFTA/NAFTA.ASP. Accessed on 14/07/15.*

74. Yip, George S. Halt, G. Tomas M., '*Total Global strategy*'. 3rd. Ed., ©2012, p. 10 reprinted by permission of Pearson Education, Inc. New York. New York.

75. Porter, Michael (1985), '*Competitive Advantage.*' The Free press

76. Ibid.

77. Grant, Robert, M (1991), '*Contemporary Strategy Analysis*'. Blackwell pp. 235.

78. Ibid.

79. *https://en.wikipedia.org/wiki/Financial_crisis_of_2007%E2%80%9308. Accessed on 01/02/16.*

80. *http://www.ft.com/cms/s/2/fe1df514-4b43-11e5-b558-8a9722977189.html#axzz3jv7GcjnV. Accessed on 12/02/16.*

81. *http://globalsherpa.org/bric-countries-brics/. Accessed on 12/02/16.*

82. *http://time.com/4106094/goldman-sachs-brics/. Accessed on 23rd. December, 2015.*

83.   Pushall Lass and Susan Hart, 'Towards Sexual Imagery in al-
        cohol   advertising: An exploratory Study in the UK, Ger-
        many and Italy.' *Journal of Marketing Management, v*ol. 20,
        Numbers 5-6, 1 June, 2004.

84.   *http://www.hongkiat.com/blog/international-marketing-*
        strategy/. Accessed on 4th. February, 2016.

85.   *http://www.econtentmag.com/Articles/Editorial/Feature/Digi-*
        tal-Advertising-Trends-You-Need-to-Know-97161.htm. Ac-
        cessed on 8th. February, 2016.

86.   *http://www.marketingjournal.org/future-of-marketing-an-*
        interview-with-philip-kotler/. Accessed on 5th. February,
        2016.

87.   *http://uk.marketo.com/infographics/the-marketing-power-*
        of-the-internet-of-things/. Accessed on 1st. February, 2016.

88.   *http://www.marketingjournal.org/marketing-and-the-inter-*
        net-of-things-are-you-ready-jamshed-dubash/. Accessed on
        5th. February, 2016.

89.   *Sultan Kermally (1996), 'Total Management Thinking.' But-*
        terworth-Heinemann.

90.   *http://www.forbes.com/sites/robertwynne/2014/07/08/the-*
        real-difference-between-pr-and-advertising-credibil-
        ity/#679a0e162270. Accessed on 3rd. February, 2016.

91.   *Economist Newspaper.* September, 23, 2000.

92.   *http://www.mckinsey.com/insights/corporate_social_respon-*
        sibility/why_philanthropy_is_r_and_d_for_business. Accessed
        on 4th. February, 2016.

93.   Michael J. Baker (2003), *'The Marketing Book.'* Butterworth-
        Heinemann

94.   Levitt, Theodore (1986)' *The Marketing Imagination.'* New
        expanded edition. Chapter 6 'Relationship management.'
        The Free Press.

95.   Payne, Andrew (1996), *'Marketing Planning for services.'*
        Butterworth-Heinemann, pp84.

96.   Payne, Andrew (1994), 'Relationship Marketing – Making the
        Customer Count.' *Managing Service quality,* vol. 4, No. 6.

97.   Reicheld, Frederick F and Sasser, earl, W (1990), 'Zero Defec-
        tions: Quality comes to services.' *Harvard Business Review,*

68 October pp105-111. ©1990 by the President and Fellows of Harvard College: all rights reserved

98.   Reicheld, Frederick F and Sasser, earl, W (1990), 'Zero Defections: Quality comes to services.'*Harvard Business Review*, 68 October pp105-111. ©1990 by the President and Fellows of Harvard College: all rights reserved.

99.   Reinartz, Werner and Kumar, V (2002), 'The mismanagement of customer loyalty.' *Harvard Business review*, July. ©2002 by the President and Fellows of Harvard College: all rights reserved.

100. Day, George and Fahey, Liam (1988), 'Valuing market strategies.' *Journal of marketing*, American Management Association, volume 52. No3, pp45-57.

101. *https://hbr.org/2015/05/a-refresher-on-economic-value-to-the-customer. Accessed on 20/01/16.*

102. *http://www.cmo.com/articles/2014/11/13/what_the_circular_ec.html. Accessed on 7th. February, 2016.*

103. *http://www.mckinsey.com/business-functions/mckinsey-digital/our-insights/digital-globalization-the-new-era-of-global-flows?cid=other-eml-alt-mgi-mck-oth-1602. Accessed on 26th. February, 2016.*

104. *http://www.fastbusiness.com.au/it-professionals/the-next-era-in-digital-transformation/. Accessed on 9th. February, 2016.*

Index